CHASING
KONA

ROB CUMMINS

ACKNOWLEDGEMENTS

There is one person without whom I never would have even started. My wife, Aisling believed I could qualify for Kona long before I or anyone else did. I started this journey with blind faith in her belief in me. Along the way she pushed, cajoled, supported, nursed and trained with me as I attempted to turn a back of the pack engine into a Kona one.

There have been days in the last half a dozen years where she pushed me out the door when I was so tired and unmotivated I wouldn't have trained otherwise. There were days when I left the house at 7am to go to the pool and arrived back to find her waiting to eat dinner and talk to me about how I got on after an eight or nine hour training day.

She pushed me past every limit I thought I had, physical, emotional and mental. She helped me become the athlete and more importantly the person I am today.

When I line up to race I start with Aisling's voice in my head telling me to "go hunt those motherfuckers down" I race to make her proud and to thank her for getting me here. I don't think there are many athletes who get to where they are alone. There is always someone behind or beside them helping, teaching or supporting. I've been lucky enough that for me that person is Aisling. She is not only an extraordinary person and athlete but also the best coach, mentor and teacher I've ever known. Not to mention friend and wife.

When I handed this book off to my editor he sent it back with the same correction throughout. (Actually there were a lot of corrections, grammar, sentence structure, spelling and worse) but what stood out the most was the fact that I constantly talk about "we" rather than "I" He had notes all the way through which started off just as corrections but eventually turned to comments which looked quite exasperated "who is we??? You and the coach??? You and Aisling??? Stick to I!!"

The thing is this is a "we" story. I don't think of me as an athlete, rather I think of us as a team, even when I'm racing alone for hours in an Ironman. When I'm racing Kona or any other Ironman I have Aisling with me inside my head and heart and I think of the results as being ours. I never want to have to admit to Ais after a race that I gave up, quit or stopped trying because that devalues her contribution to getting me to the start line.

I'm always racing with the thought that I want Ais to be proud but also that I want to be able to stand in front of her after a race and tell her I raced honestly, that I emptied the tank, that I never once gave in to the hurt and quit. The result is much less important than the way that it was achieved. A Kona slot won comfortably by drafting on the bike isn't worth one tenth of the one that's fought for tooth and nail right to the finish line. I want her not to be proud of my result, but of how I achieved it. I want to have earned whatever the outcome is.

This book might look like it's my story but really it's ours. You will inevitably find places where I still talk about "we" instead of "I" I just didn't think it was an "I" moment (To Dermott my editor I apologise) but the truth is that this is a story of us, not me. If it's confusing I apologise.

This is my first book and as such I am learning a new craft. Any mistakes are mine and I hope you can enjoy it regardless.

Oh and for all of you non Irish readers Aisling is pronounced Ash-ling or Ais is pronounced Ash. Ais and Aisling are both the same person.

There were plenty of people who helped me get to Kona. Coaches, training partners, family and friends. There have been just as many who encouraged and helped with this book. I'm not going to name them all here as I'm sure I'll forget someone.

I hope you know who you are and how much you helped.

Thank you.

Rob C

TABLE OF CONTENTS

Chapter 1 Bolton August 2011 1

Chapter 2 Smoker... 13

Chapter 3 Discovering cycling 17

Chapter 4 Falling in love with the bike 21

Chapter 5 Hooked on Iron 37

Chapter 6 Losing my triathlon virginity - Dublin city triathlon 2003 .. 43

Chapter 7 Learning to swim - Winter 2005......................... 49

Chapter 8 A mountain bike race ....
.... 57

Chapter 9 Ironman France June 2008 65

Chapter 10 Life changes and Ironman Switzerland 2009 69

Chapter 11 100k Ultra... 71

Chapter 12 A coach and belief 77

Chapter 13 Simple not easy.. 83

Chapter 14 Training camps, pushing limits......................... 89

Chapter 15 The Last Push – Hell of The West Triathlon – Kilkee, 2011
.... 93

Chapter 16 August 2011 Ironman U.K Bolton 2011 97

Chapter 17 Not so invincible after all 107

Chapter 18 Ironman Florida 2011 111

Chapter 19 Off season, Ultra, Half Iron 117

Chapter 20 Race the Rás 2012 – prologue: pre-race rituals 123

Chapter 21 Ironman UK (IMUK), July 2012..................... 127

Chapter 22 Kona 2012 –The trip and race week............... 135

Chapter 23 Ironman World Championship, Kona Hawaii 2012....... 143

Chapter 24 Becoming an athlete 149

CHAPTER 1
BOLTON – AUGUST 2011

My legs hurt. My neck and back both ache. My ass is in a lot of discomfort. I shift in the saddle as I slide forward, dropping down two gears and spinning my legs faster, trying to relax the muscles that are overworking and desperately trying to get some relief from the pain. I'm trying to hold my average speed constant, something that is becoming increasingly difficult to do. It's getting harder to keep pushing as I tire. I think of my coach back at home watching the results popping up live on line and I wonder what he's thinking. When we started working together he didn't believe I could do this and only took me on as a client reluctantly. It's been one of the things that has kept me motivated over the last four months. . . the thought that I'd prove him wrong. I shift back up a gear. I accelerate. I hold on to the hurt. I won't slow down. I won't fail. I look ahead and see someone in the distance and focus on them.

I remember Aisling's advice to focus on the next one and go after him, then the next and the next. Her exact words were to 'hunt those motherfuckers down'. I can hear her now in my mind telling me to push, to stretch myself – to reach further than I believe possible. And that makes me shift another gear and push even harder. I look up the road and work out the time gap to the next athlete. He's just over one minute ahead. The road rises a little and I shift up a couple of gears and get up out of the saddle, stretching my back and giving my aching legs something else to shout about. I settle into a rhythm on the climb, the bike swaying in time to my pedal stroke. My world shrinks down to just the spot ahead of my front wheel and for a while the pain fades into the background. I shift gear again and accelerate. My legs protest slightly then decide they will cooperate and settle. And then I've found that sweet spot below my threshold that I feel I could hold on to all day. It seems like I'm dancing. I feel light on the pedals. For a moment it's effortless. I look ahead and I'm surprised to see that rider is now right in front of me. I've closed the gap quickly. I pull out and ride by him. He's labouring on the short hill and I realise that he's blown his lights. He's cooked. Probably started too fast and now he's paying the price. I flick the fingers of my left hand in greeting as I overtake. He doesn't respond. He's inside his own head and doesn't seem aware of me.

I crest the rise and drop gingerly back into the saddle, squirming and shifting around to find some position that doesn't hurt. There isn't one, so I push on regardless. The pain in my legs and everywhere else is back. The brief respite while I was out of the saddle is over and it's back to business. Another rider is visible in the distance and again I remember Aisling's words 'hunt that motherfucker'. It's become a mantra playing over and over in my head, distracting me from the pain, giving me another focus and he comes closer to me. I drop another gear and accelerate hard to make the pass. I want to make sure he doesn't try to follow and a part of me wants to demoralise him. No not demoralise, destroy! I want to make sure that there's no chance that he even tries to race me. I want him to feel so weak that he quits. I want to crush him.

Outside of racing and off the bike I'm not like this, and I never admit to having these feelings except to one or two people. I'm afraid that I'll be called an arsehole. I'll be judged for it and that people will think that this is my usual mind-set. But right now I'm looking up the road for the next target. It takes a couple of minutes but I see someone in the distance. It looks like a woman. She must be one of the pros. I've passed a couple of female professionals so far, which is the only indication that I'm near the front end of the field and the fact that the field has thinned out considerably. The riders I'm catching are further and further apart as I move through.

I glance down to check my average speed and it looks good. I'm almost on target and haven't slowed down at all in the second half of the race I take encouragement from this fact and push again, despite the increasingly loud protests from my legs. I round a corner and come upon the female rider. She's slowed a bit and as I ride past I look at the name on her number and realise that it's Desiree Flicker. She was in the pre- race news as being the favourite to win the women's race. I feel a huge swell of emotion and excitement rising inside me. Initially try to suppress it, before giving in and embracing it. If I've just passed the favourite in the women's race then I'm probably much closer to the front of the field than I had thought. It's the first time that I really start to believe that I can do this and the feelings of excitement, mixed with relief, are bursting within me.

The pain suddenly disappears and I push harder. I'm riding on a huge wave of emotion. I use the feelings as fuel and push harder. There's not far to go now and as I rise out of the saddle to start the short rise to the turn-off point I again feel like I'm dancing and have to hold myself back a little. There's a big crowd at the turn-off point and I get a huge cheer when they realise that I'm almost finished and not going out to start another lap. The shouting and cheering lifts me further and I look around and smile at them. I try to burn as much of this into my memory and try to store the emotions to fire me up for the marathon still to come.

It's only a couple of kilometres to the second transition and the end of the bike leg and I ride in fast. The crowd is a little smaller here but the noise is fantastic. I've slipped my feet out of the bike shoes and am pedalling with my feet on top of them. I turn the last corner and see the dismount line some 50m ahead. I don't slow down and the marshals are getting a little worried that I might not stop. They wave and shout, pointing at the white line on the ground. In one fluid and well practised move I rise out of the saddle, swing my right leg over the bike and only a couple of feet before the line I drop off the other pedal at over 20kph and land at a run just like I've done in countless short course races.

My legs scream in disbelief at the stupidity of this idea and simply refuse to cooperate. I almost crash to the ground right there in front of everyone but somehow manage to stay upright and turn right into transition. I'm shocked to see that it's almost empty which means I'm right up at the front of the field. In my mind I'd visualised racing and crossing the line and qualifying many times in training but I somehow had overlooked the fact that to be competitive in my age group would mean being competitive overall. It's one of those really obvious things that I should have been expecting but I was shocked by it. I guess a big part a part of me never really believed it would happen. It hits me again and I start to believe I can race at this level. I'm doing it, I'm actually doing it! The thought keeps going round in my head. I've dreamed of this for years but it's one thing having a dream. It's another actually making it happen. Until this precise moment I never really believed it was possible.

I hand off my bike and marvel once more at all the empty racks. My legs still aren't working properly though and it's a lumpy, uncoordinated run through transition. I enter the hall where our run bags are lined up on the floor where we left them. I run straight to mine, but I'm directed over to the side of the hall to a row of benches. I sit down heavily. I sort of collapse really, my quads screaming in protest.

I lean over to pull on my shoes and my hamstring goes into the most awful cramp. My leg shoots out in front of me and for the second time in a matter of minutes I almost land face down. I twist and try to stretch out. One of the marshals starts coming over towards me to see if I'm alright and I wave her off. The cramp subsides but I still haven't got my shoe on and I'm afraid that if I try again it will spasm out of control, landing me on the floor scrabbling around like an upended beetle. The clock is ticking and the urgency is building. My stomach is tightening into a hard ball of tension. I reach down as quickly as I can, bending my leg at the same time. I can feel the muscle pulling into a savage cramp again and I pull my shoe on viciously and straighten my leg, stretching it out and grimacing against the pain of the partially cramping hamstring. I reach into my bag, grabbing my hat and run belt. The marshal takes my bag and tells me to go. I hobble into a shambling run out the door. In all my transition time was one minute forty seconds. It felt like five times that.

It's a downhill start out of transition and I concentrate on small fast steps. I'm trying to get my legs working. There's very little spectator support out here and I take the time to settle myself and try to find a rhythm. I pull on my hat as I run and fasten my run belt around my waist, adjusting it until it sits low on my hips and doesn't bounce.

I have a pacing plan that I'm determined to stick to rigidly. I'm aiming on running easy for the first 10k then build to as fast a cruise as I can maintain for the middle 20k section then hang on for dear life for the last 12k. I'm reminded of a quote I heard somewhere that goes 'If you want to make god laugh tell him about your plans'. I decide to keep them to myself for the moment. As and the coaches both warned me several times, I should not start too fast, regardless of how good I'm feeling. I check my Garmin and the first kilometre is fast – a little too fast – so I back off. It feels easy and I settle into a groove almost immediately. I check my Garmin again and the second kilometre is still too fast. I back off a bit more and this pace is starting to feel slow. I'm getting that slightly panicked feeling again in my stomach. I look over my shoulder feeling like I'm going so slowly that I must be caught by the whole field. I expect to see a stampede of tall, fit, tanned triathletes bearing down on me, but there's only a couple of guys strung out along the road. I turn back to the task at hand and start to look ahead thinking about 'hunting those motherfuckers down'.

I feel like I'm straining against an invisible leash. My legs saying 'fuck it let's go', my head saying 'don't be a clown'. I pass the three-kilometre marker. My legs have settled after the cycling and every part of me is grateful to be upright and not crouched down over my tri-bars. I shake my arms, working out the stiffness from the bike and my Garmin beeps to tell me I've done another kilometre. That was quick, I think. My pace is now bang on target but it still feels way too easy. I tell myself to have patience but the fear of being caught is building inside me again. I look over my shoulder, but there's still no one close to me. As I turn and look ahead I realise I'm gaining on the guy in front. I check my pace again and I'm still on target. Beep. The Garmin tells me that's another kilometre done. I'm feel like I'm gliding, it feels so easy and I want so badly to stride out and push the pace. I still feel like I'm straining on an imaginary leash. I'm running alongside a canal and there are no spectators here – just the runner up ahead and one quite a bit behind. The sun is out and I can taste the salt from hours of sweat on my lips. The Garmin beeps again, six kilometres. I look down to be sure. It only feels like seconds since the last one. I look ahead and now the runner in front is only a couple of metres ahead. I pick up my pace just a little. Just to make the pass I tell myself, then I'll slow back down. God it feels good to open it up. I glide by and as I pass I pat him on the back and offer a word of encouragement. He tells me I'm flying and to keep it up. I should slow back down to my target pace but I don't. It feels too good so I just push on. It's completely effortless. I cruise the length of the canal loving the feeling of the sun on my skin and the silence. The faster pace has my breathing a little quicker at first but as I've sometimes found the body adapts to the workload after a couple of minutes.

Sure enough everything settles again. My breathing slows and I'm holding the faster pace with what seems like no greater effort than before. I reach the end of the canal section and there's a steep hill up to the main part of the course. I love running hills and normally hit the gas hard pushing right up to the red line and holding it there before backing off over the crest and recovering on the downhill. I don't think that will work in an Ironman marathon. At least I don't have the nerve to test the theory so I slow right down. Just as I'm reaching the halfway point of the hill a guy comes flying past me. Jesus he looks strong, I think to myself and almost give in to the urge to chase. I tell myself that he's either going too hard in which case he'll blow up and I'll catch him or he's just faster than me in which case I won't. Either way I just have to run my own race. As it turns out I see him again in about fifteen minutes, vomiting at the side of the road.

I crest the hill and came onto the lapped part of the run course. There are more spectators here but the course itself is almost empty. I still can't believe that I'm up here with the leading athletes. It was exactly as I had dreamed on all of those long training rides and runs when I had endless hours to imagine what it would feel like. I never imagined it would feel like this. Never in my wildest dreams did I think I would run like this. I tell myself to enjoy it while I can.

I see an Irish flag up ahead and I accelerate a little, the excitement driving me on. I'm vaguely aware somewhere in the back of my mind that I might be going too fast but then I pass the Irish fans and they recognise the Wheelworx kit and they give me a big shout. It gives me a huge lift and I pick up the pace a little more, feeling incredible. I'm cruising, feeling like I can do this all day and although it isn't quite as effortless as it had been, it's very comfortable and still the Garmin keeps beeping telling me I've done another kilometre and again I'm surprised at how quickly it happens and I also keep on ignoring the voice in the back of my head that's telling me I might be going too fast. I had practised my nutrition in training and so far it has been working perfectly. I drop down the hill into Bolton city centre for the first time and the crowds and the noise are building.

Ais had told me before that she smiles at the spectators on the course and acknowledges their support and in response they often cheered harder and smiled back. She said to do it and that I would get a good lift from them. I did it from the start of the first lap and I couldn't believe the buzz I got from every smile. The spectators seemed to be getting as much of a kick out of it as I was and whenever they saw me coming on later laps they shouted louder and every time it lifted me a little more.

Bolton is mostly an out and back lap, so you can see the guys ahead of you coming in the opposite direction. I had started counting as soon as I got onto the lap, wondering how far up the field I actually was. I think I missed some through the town and at the aid stations but I was well below 50th at the turn around. This gave me another boost. I was running strongly now and well into what I considered the main part of the marathon. I was still moving faster than I was supposed to be according to the plan, but I had thrown caution out the window quite some distance back and was flying firmly by the seat of my pants. Plans be damned! I again thought of the coach watching the tracker at home and if he had been happy with my pacing earlier on I could see him cursing at my stupidity now as I crossed each timing mat further and further ahead of schedule. I became more and more determined not to fall apart. I wasn't going to give him, or give anyone else the satisfaction of saying 'I told you so'. The more I thought of it the more determined I became. And my determination turned to anger at his inability to believe in me, so I ran faster. I passed the half waypoint in the marathon, running harder and allowing the anger to sit in the back of my head. Feeding on it, knowing that I was using it to fuel my effort. A part of me knew it was a bad idea. But I ignored that part.

I hadn't seen Ais since the swim start. She was racing as well and I had been looking forward to seeing her for hours. We knew that the first time we would see each other was on the run course. She joined the lap just as I was passing that point and she was flying. I have this image in my head of a cartoon character running around a corner, arms windmilling, all leaned over and skidding almost out of control. That's what she looked like. Oh! and with the biggest smile you've ever seen. Ais loves running and she's savagely good at it. Especially if that running is insanely long or comes after a 3.8k swim and 180k bike race?. She laugh-shouted a greeting as she ran past me, going in the opposite direction. She was charging up through the field and looking like the happiest person on the course.. My emotions in that moment flip-flopped from the anger that had fuelled me for the last couple of kilometres and transformed into massive happiness and excitement.

I was again running on the buzz of the day. I was floating. I was cruising. My effort level was rising along with my speed but I thought I still had it under control. The 25, 26, 27 and 28k markers all came and went with the same speed as the earlier part of the marathon, but now the course was fuller as more and more people started their run. I was enjoying the buzz from the athletes and supporters and was passing and lapping people constantly. The earlier loneliness of the course had been replaced with an almost party-like atmosphere in and around the town. I felt invincible. I knew that this probably wouldn't last, so I kept on telling myself to enjoy it.

The last part of my nutrition plan had been to take an energy drink I had used before. It was high in sugar and caffeine and I found it gave me an almighty kick. I'd carried two small 125ml bottles of it since the second transition, with the plan of taking it at thirty kilometres or a little earlier if needed. I was almost at the 30k mark and I downed one almost in one go. I waited a couple of minutes before taking the second one. My legs were getting sore but I was still moving well. Any second now the energy drink would kick in and I'd take off like a rocket. At least that's what I told myself. It didn't take too long to have an effect but not quite what I'd planned. I got a stitch in my side. The pain grew and I tried stretching while I was running. Probably looking drunk as I leaned crazily to one side with my arm reaching way above my head. It had no effect. I tried backing off for a minute. No effect, except for a growing fear that I was going to get caught. This forced me to speed up again, despite the growing discomfort. But the stitch became more painful the harder I pushed. To make matters worse my legs had decided to join in and let me know how supremely pissed off they were with the day's abuse. I focused on the spectators, looking for a smile or a cheer. I found one and then looked for another, desperately hoping to distract myself from the mounting pain. My head started to drop and I was slowing. I heard a shout, but didn't look up. They shouted again and I looked to the side of the road and a girl who'd been cheering hard all day shouted that I was on my last lap and that I was flying. 'Push hard', she shouted while she smiled broadly at me, so I again piled on the pressure. I stopped feeling sorry for myself and focused on the next athlete and went after him. Then the next. I started to pat them on the back again every time I made a pass, as I had done earlier in the day when I had still felt good. It took my focus off my own suffering and I heard the Garmin beep again. Another kilometre done and then I was dropping down the hill into Bolton for the last time and I let gravity drag me faster, despite the screaming pain in my legs and side. It was only a couple of minutes now. 'You can suck it up and hold on to this pain for a couple of minutes', I mentally shouted at myself. The crowds were huge in town by now and the roars were deafening as I got into the last mile. I could feel the emotion building and I didn't fight it. I could feel tears building. I still didn't know if I'd done enough to win, but I knew that my time was faster than last year's qualifying time so I kept on hoping. I dared not slow down and pushed hard all the way to the line. I struggled to contain the emotion as I crossed the finish where I staggered to a halt, supported by the marshals as they warmly welcomed me and put the medal around my neck.

That buzz at the finish line of an Ironman is still one of the most incredible feelings I've ever experienced and it doesn't seem to diminish no matter how many times I re-live it in my mind.

As soon as I stopped I wanted to lie down. And I didn't mean the normal process of leaning back sitting then kicking my legs up and stretching out. I wanted to go from vertical to horizontal instantly, with no time in between. I briefly gave in to the urge and started to crumple before the marshal beside me grabbed my arm. I was both grateful and a bit pissed off. Grateful of the help and support, but a little annoyed because I really did want to lie down really badly. He helped me into the recovery tent, where he put me into a chair. I only took a minute to get myself together. Then I struggled to my feet and went to find the results. I still had no idea if I'd qualified for Kona or what position I'd come. I went back to the finish line where the race director told me I could get the results online. I thanked him and hobbled to the baggage area to get my phone and clean clothes.

I switched the phone on with badly shaking hands. I was getting cold and weak. I opened the tracker knowing that there was seven provisional qualifying slots in my age group. At nine hours forty-nine I was almost twenty minutes inside my time target, but qualifying was based on position not time, so I still had no idea where I stood. The page loaded slowly and it said I was fifth. I knew I had qualified!

For the second time in ten minutes my legs almost collapsed under me. The massive rolling feeling of euphoria and relief was unlike anything I'd ever experienced. I immediately headed back out to the course to see Ais and tell her. It was bursting out of me, I could barely contain my excitement. I waited for her on a corner, hardly able to stand, but definitely unable to get up unaided if I sat on the kerb, so I stood. Tears of relief were close but I held them back. I wasn't going to start crying in public.

Then I saw her and waved. She was still smiling her huge beautiful smile and she was flying. At that stage she was easily the fastest person on the course. I shouted 'Fifth! I did it, I qualified!' She squealed with delight, did a little jump and dance all without breaking stride and ran on laughing. She did the short lap around town before heading back onto the course. I waited and watched her go out to start another lap. I rang my folks and told them that I'd done it, that I'd qualified. They were delighted but I felt couldn't stay on the phone very long. I was losing control and I could feel all of the pent up emotions rushing to the surface. I made an excuse and said I'd call later. I walked away from the crowds and found a small quiet side street. I sat in a doorway and let the feelings I'd been barely able to hold back gush out of me. Tears streamed down my face as I sat there, somehow smiling. After a couple of minutes I took out my phone and texted the coach.

'Fifth' was all I said. His reply was like a kick in the stomach. 'The trackers were wrong, the updated results have you as eighth'. I almost got sick. The euphoria and relief turned to a small hard knot of hot acid tension in my stomach. All I could think was how am I going to tell Ais? I couldn't believe it. I checked the updated results and I was eight. Fuck! I went back to the finish area and tried to eat something. I met a friend who had also raced. He was in my age group and had beaten me by finishing fourth. He had seen my result and my face and knew what I was thinking. 'I'm not taking my slot for Kona. I can't race there this year. It will roll down so you will go to Hawaii,' he said.

I couldn't believe it. It was like being on a roller coaster. One minute

I thought I'd done it. The next I knew I hadn't and then I thought I still might have a chance. The only problem is that I wasn't to know for certain until the following day at the awards ceremony.

CHAPTER 2
SMOKER

Most children grow up wanting to be something special. A star footballer, Formula 1 driver, championship golfer, ballerina, princess, film star, professional cyclist or maybe an Olympian. For most of us these aspirations remain dreams, despite realising at some stage, perhaps in our teenage years or early adulthood that we will never be the next Michael Schumacher, David Beckham or Marilyn Monroe. Even so, many of us never fully let go of these dreams of youth. Some escape reality by heading out on a Sunday to the golf course, while others pull on a pair of runners and shorts and knock out a twenty-mile run.

I started sport relatively late in life. I was almost 27 years old when I quit a ten-year, forty to fifty cigarettes a day habit. I tried a number of sports in school, including football, boxing and swimming, but most of my efforts only lasted as long as the compulsory PE class and even then I was pretty awful. It turned out that my real skills were in underage smoking, drinking and getting into trouble. I was a difficult teenager and my parents had a hard time keeping me in line.

I don't have a sad story to use as an excuse behind my troublemaking. There was no broken home or abusive parents to blame. There was nothing to excuse me becoming a total pain in the ass. Mam and Dad were as good as I could ever have asked for as parents. They have always been quite exceptional. I just didn't see that at the time. In fact it took me a long time to realise that they were far from ordinary. Dad was a very successful self- made businessman and my inspiration to start my own business. From the time I was quite young I wanted to 'be the boss' just like him.

As we grew up and moved on with our own lives his business allowed him the freedom to try new challenges. It was his nature to face all challenges head on – bringing him right to the limits of his ability. At some stage he decided that golf was not for him. He started on a series of daunting projects, including becoming a crew member in a round the world yacht race. This was despite the fact that he knew nothing about boats or sailing and that he was the oldest member of the crew. He was over 60 years old at the time, but he was one of the fittest and strongest in the team. He has trekked the Inca trail to Machu Picchu in the Andes of Peru and both Mam and Dad have spent time on charity projects building schools in Lesotho in southern Africa. They even climbed Mount Kilimanjaro successfully at their first attempt. Probably Dad's most impressive sporting achievement, however, was at the age of 72, when he took up running for the first time in his life and in less than nine months ran his first marathon. Mam is also a champion ten-pin bowler and even in her sixties makes national and international teams, despite having only taken it up less than ten years ago. I suppose when I look at my own activities now from the point of view of my parents' exceptional achievements I was always likely to set high, difficult targets for myself.

After school I gladly left sports behind and spent a dozen or so years abusing my body and health. I was smoking, eating junk food, drinking and living a completely sedentary lifestyle. I was heading into my late twenties and I couldn't walk up a flight of stairs without becoming badly winded. I had tried to quit smoking dozens of times, each time lasting anything from an hour to several months. But I believed people were either smokers or they weren't and if you were, it was for life. I felt like I was trapped, never to kick the habit.

In 1998, after another Christmas of hangovers, colds, flu and an ever-worsening smokers cough, I along with a large part of the population, decided to set 1 January 1999 as a new beginning. I had never really bothered with any New Year's resolutions before, but I was desperate. I had tried all the usual remedies, like nicotine patches, gum and willpower, but none had worked, so I decided to try something new.

Being a reader I went looking for a book about how to stop smoking. I knew it would change my life if I became a non-smoker. I knew I would feel better, have more energy and maybe even try some exercise. Despite not having any interest in physical exercise as a teenager, I was envious of those who were strong and fit enough to run. But to be honest I had no idea just how liberating it would be. When you finally do something you have always seen as being impossible it changes you as a person.

I discovered a book by Alan Carr called *The Only Way To Stop Smoking*. At the time I was a voracious reader. I had plenty of time, aside from work and family commitments. I didn't really have any other hobbies and usually got through books in hours or days, rarely taking more than a week to get through one. This one, however, was different. It took me over three months to read. I realised it was working after a couple of days and I slowed myself down, stupidly hanging on to the cigarettes just a little longer. As much as I wanted to stop I was afraid to do so. In the end I finished the book and smoked my last cigarette on St Patricks Day, 17 March 1999.

Ironically at about the same time, in another world, Aisling my wife – whom I didn't yet know and wouldn't meet for another nine years – discovered and read the same book. Aisling being a more leisurely reader would normally take weeks rather than days to get through a book, but it had the opposite effect on her. She sensed freedom from cigarettes coming the minute she started to read and didn't put the book down for three days. I believe it was at a time that she would now call a PB (personal best) At this point she, like me, was a non- smoker. I love her description of how it felt to be free of cigarettes. 'It was like coming up out of the trenches.'

It opened up a whole new world for Aisling. She started to run, and in what was to become her standard modus operandi, she dived straight in to the deep end, entering and finishing her first marathon later that year in Dublin. And that was only the beginning. The deep end was not quite deep enough, or maybe just the standard marathon of 26.2 miles wasn't long enough for her, so she immediately moved up to ultramarathon distance races. An 'ultra' is anything longer than a marathon. Some of the normal or traditional distances are fifty and one hundred kilometres, fifty and one hundred miles or double and triple marathons etc., but are not limited to these distances and some are much, much longer.

Ultras are also measured in time. Twelve, twenty-four and even forty-eight hour races while not exactly mainstream are considered quite 'normal' in ultra-running. They are often raced on a 400m athletics track. The athletes all start together and whoever covers the most distance in the time wins.

If I was to get all mystical and hippyish I might take the view that we might never have met and I most likely wouldn't have taken this Ironman and Kona journey if it was not for those two separate events over fifteen years ago. It's funny how a tiny event, decision or change of direction can lead one to a completely different reality. That is something that I've learned, again and again. Seemingly small changes in direction can open up new worlds.

On the subject of ultras, one of the funny things I've come across since taking up Ironman distance racing is that ultra-runners often think we're mad and maybe a bit superhuman – what with all that swimming, cycling and then running a whole marathon at the end. However, Ironman triathletes think ultra-runners are just as crazy. Maybe there is a touch of craziness in what we do, pushing our bodies up to and beyond what we and others think our limits are, but I don't think so. I think we are the sane ones. I think maybe everyone else is crazy!

CHAPTER 3
DISCOVERING CYCLING
– APRIL 1999

I didn't know it in April 1999, but my life was about to take a new direction. I'd started my own business the previous August when I opened a small bicycle shop and had rewarded myself with a mountain bike after about a month, as a prize for staying off cigarettes. My first proper ride took place one evening along with the guy who worked for me at that time. He had been asking me for ages to come mountain biking, telling me I'd love the buzz and the adrenaline rush. I eventually gave in very reluctantly, thinking I wasn't fit enough for it and we drove up to the trails one evening after work. The plan was to ride up the hard packed gravel road to the top where the real fun bit would start when we turned and headed back down the 'single track', whatever that the hell that was.

I lasted less than five minutes of climbing before having to stop. My breathing was ragged and I was coughing hard, one of the consequences of being a long-time heavy smoker. I stopped and caught my breath and went again. The exertion started a racking cough, which brought up dark brown lumps of phlegm. I only managed a couple of hundred metres at a time before having to stop and recover. About half way to the top I had had enough and said I was going back down. I was disgusted and ashamed of myself and wanted to quit. This wasn't fun and I couldn't do it. 'This mountain biking lark is a load of shite', I said. It was easier to stop if it was for a reason other than that I was a failure . . . it was easier to blame something else.

'It's just a couple of hundred metres more and we can join the single track trail back down where it crosses the fire road. You'll love it', he said again.

I was far from convinced but gave in and pedalled on very slowly, finally getting to the gap in the trees. I was then given some brief instruction about not being over zealous in my use of the front brake, hanging my backside off the back of the saddle on the steeper bits so as not to go tipping over the handlebars, not fighting the bike and told to just enjoy it. We then turned left and dropped into the forest. He let go of the brakes and flicked the bike around trees, over rocks and roots and disappeared into the distance as if by magic. I tried to keep up, pushing harder and harder. My eyes were streaming, my hands and arms aching, and my pounding legs were like jelly. Adrenaline dumped itself into my system, causing a rush unlike anything I'd ever experienced. At the same time muscles that I'd never used before and certainly had never abused in such a way were letting it be known in no uncertain fashion that they had a very short tolerance for this sort of messing about.

Despite or probably because of the pain, fatigue and terror, I rode down on the biggest buzz I'd ever experienced. My friend waited patiently at every junction and led the way again and again. What was eyeballs out, terrifying and suicidally fast for me was obviously very pedestrian for anyone with any basic level of mountain biking competence, never mind someone who was a very experienced and fairly successful cross country racer. He not only had skill, strength and fitness by the bucket load, but was also incredibly patient and brought me back in one piece to where we had started the trail.

After the tortuously slow journey to the top of the trail we arrived back down far too quickly and I think he was surprised with my reaction, considering fifteen minutes before I'd wanted to fire the bike into the nearest ditch. 'Let's go again! Now! That was savage!' I sounded like an over-excited six-year-old. And just like that I'd turned onto a new path. I didn't know it at the time but as a result of that first mountain bike ride my life would become so completely different as to be unrecognisable. I would become a different person with a very different life.

Over the next couple of months I drifted in and out of mountain biking. I was a very typical beginner, not only to cycling but also to sport. I quite enjoyed it while I was actually doing it but often lacked the motivation to drag myself away from the television or play station. I always had at my disposal any number of the usual excuses we give ourselves to avoid going out the door. It's cold, wet, I can't find my bike shoes, and look now I've spent so much time faffing around I don't have time to drive to the mountain, ride and drive back. I was still a long way from being fit enough to cycle the six or seven kilometres to and from the trails, as well as doing a spin up there.

I stuck with it however, even though my outings were infrequent. Over time I gradually became fitter, pushing myself further, doing longer and longer spins and even had a go at cross country racing. I came last at my first race and wasn't so excited by it. I believe my thoughts were along the lines of 'this is the stupidest idea and the stupidest sport and what a complete load of shite and I'm never doing this again' as I was lapped several times. The fast guys at the front seemed like they were from a different planet and we were only racing in the entry-level 'Sports' category. I never believed I would be at the front of a race, never mind moving up to the 'Expert' or 'Elite' categories. Despite my mid-race tantrum I did go back and did move up to the top third of the field over the next season or two. The guys at the very front were still very much on another level and it was so far away from where I was as to be something I believed I could never achieve, and they still lapped me every time.

CHAPTER 4
FALLING IN LOVE WITH THE BIKE

After a while I had decided to give road cycling a go and bought an entry level racing bike. As much as I enjoyed the mountain biking it just took too much time out of your day. An hour's riding on the trails either required a 20-40 minute drive both ways or close to an hour each way if I chose to ride there. The initial attraction to a road bike was that I was 'there' the minute I walked out my front door and sat on the bike. In the beginning it was only meant to be as a way of training for mountain biking but gradually I got sucked in and became a roadie.

One of my first memories and I think one of the things that made me stick with cycling was going out and learning how to 'ride on a wheel'. You ride really close behind the rider in front, staying in their slipstream so you aren't working as hard. I went out for a spin one day with a much stronger rider and he had been explaining it to me but could see it wasn't really hitting home, so he decided to show me what exactly it was and how much of a buzz it could be. We had been out for an hour or so, which back then was a fairly standard spin for me. Anything over ninety minutes would be a long ride. It's funny how your perspective on things shifts completely when you change your routine. I wouldn't even consider an hour's ride training now – it's just too short to have any real benefit.

Anyway, back to the 'ride on a wheel' spin. We were close to where we would split up and head off in different directions to go home, but the last stretch of road before the turn was almost flat. Almost, it had just the tiniest drop in elevation the whole way, the surface was good, plus we had a light tailwind. We normally rode two abreast so we could chat but he said to me that he was going to go on the front and pick up the pace. I was to get right behind him and stay as close to his wheel as possible.

'Like inches close, not feet and don't fall back. And push hard all the way', he said. 'Ok', I said, not really knowing what was coming but I trusted him and he said it would be fun. He accelerated slowly and pulled in front of me letting his pace settle a bit as I speeded up to get onto his wheel. Then he steadily but constantly picked up the pace, looking over his shoulder every ten to fifteen seconds to make sure I was still there. The speed crept up and up. I was glued to his wheel and getting sucked along much faster than I could have gone alone. My breathing very quickly became harsh and my legs were burning, but I was also getting a big blast of adrenaline from the speed. He had us up over 45kph and closing in on 50kph. I was rapidly approaching my limit but didn't want to get dropped so I pushed harder and my breathing became more and more ragged. My legs got heavier and heavier and I started to drift off the wheel. Just one foot, then two, then as I came out of the slipstream the wind hit me and almost like someone hit the brakes I went from flying to freewheeling and almost to a stop in seconds. I was gasping, lungs and legs burning and my heart was hammering. Tears were streaming from my eyes because of the force of the wind.

But overriding all of that was the fact that I couldn't stop grinning. The adrenaline and endorphins were coursing through me like a drug. Just like the first time I'd gone mountain biking and discovered an adrenaline high. I'd found it again and I was hooked this time.

I have a tendency to overdo things a little sometimes. At the start, something becomes all- consuming and I can get what Dad would call a 'fire in my belly' for it. Cycling was very like that. I didn't just have a fire in my belly, but rather I sort of fell in love with it. I'm guessing you'll only understand that if you're a cyclist. How can you fall in love with an inanimate object like a bicycle? I suppose people might understand this phenomenon in relation to a particular sport. Having fallen in love with the bike it became so much more than an object. It very quickly became part of my identity.

Quite quickly I saw myself as a cyclist, which made me a bit odd in the eyes of most of the general population – being the guy who goes out in public in multi-coloured, skintight Lycra. All of a sudden I found this whole world with its own history, epic races, suffering, heroism and glory and I felt very much part of it. It didn't matter that I only rode a couple of times a week or that I wasn't very fit. I still felt I fitted in to the cycling world.

Out on the road other cyclists would nod or flick a tiny wave as they passed in the opposite direction. I still to this day get a kick from that. So I started reading books and watching the races on television. I bought all the magazines and of course I owned a bicycle shop, so I met other cyclists every day. Most of them had way more knowledge and experience of cycling than I had, so I was like a sponge, taking in all their stories. I simply couldn't get enough talk about bicycles and the wonderful sport of cycling. Because the business was still fairly new and small and not too busy, there was always time to talk and drink coffee.

As I followed my new path into the world of road cycling, so too did the shop. What had started out as a local bike shop with kids' bikes, tricycles and cheap basic adult mountain bikes, very slowly started to change. Gradually as I learnt about the sport and the bikes I added higher priced and more specialist stock. Of course in the beginning I knew very little about this side of the business and made lots of mistakes, but gradually as the local cyclists saw better bikes, clothing and components appearing, they started dropping in and because the shop was small and the 'workshop' was right there out on the floor – actually down the back – I would often find myself working on a bike and when they realised that I was a fellow cyclist conversations would start and often friendships would follow.

I've made a lot of friends through not only the shop but also through my increasing involvement with cycling. In my experience most, if not all cyclists, love bike shops. I love the way they smell, being mostly the smell of rubber from the tyres. It was that smell that greeted me every day that I owned that first shop and to this day whenever I walk into any bike shop and get that smell it feels like I'm coming home. Cyclists love looking at, touching, feeling and picking up the bikes, marvelling at how light and gorgeous they are. They love all the 'kit' the technical clothing, all with their own story of what they do and why they are the best. Carbon fibre bottle cages that weigh only grams and elicit 'oohhs' and' aahhhs' when they're picked up. Expensive carbon fibre wheels that cost thousands of euro a pair are probably the most coveted upgrade you could buy. I loved all the toys and was surrounded by them all day. I was also constantly meeting people with exactly the same passion and love for bikes and the sport of cycling.

So with a 'fire in my belly' I had access to great bikes and cyclists and now I was discovering a love of training. But on the other hand I had two young kids and my own business to run, not to mention the damage caused to my body by ten years of smoking. So I was never going to turn professional but I still wanted to give road racing a go.

I had no idea what to do other than ride. Of course I read the magazines and some books but I didn't really know anything about how to train properly. I needed to find ways of getting the miles in without it either causing friction at home or causing problems in work, so I started commuting on the bike. I didn't live very far from the shop so I would extend my ride as often as possible, trying to get an hour in for at least one of the spins if I could. I started doing a longer two or three-hour ride on Sunday before opening the shop at noon. I kept it up and I trained hard through the autumn and into winter. As this was the first time I'd ever trained properly I saw gains very quickly. You always do if you're starting from as low a base as I was and you just train consistently. Most of my riding was done alone but I'd occasionally meet a couple of friends to share the Sunday spin.

One Sunday I was out with a group with which I didn't usually train. One of the guys was a customer and had been asking me for a while to go out with this group on some of their training rides. Up to now I'd been afraid of not being able to keep up and had always refused, making various excuses. But by now I'd been training well for a while and was feeling fitter so I finally gave in. There was a group of maybe ten of us who showed up, all of us training to race the following season.

Some of the lads had a season or two under their belts, some had been at it for years and were with this group for an easy spin I guessed, while a couple of us were just starting. We rolled out and I sat into the group. If you haven't been on a club ride you've probably seen them while you've been out driving, usually riding in a double line in at the side of the road.

While you're in the group with other riders in front you're in the draft. You get sucked along by the riders in front who are 'in the wind'. They are usually working at least 20-30 per cent harder than someone in the middle of the group which is sheltered. The group rotates constantly so that no one or two riders have to do all the work.

Sometimes being on the front is called pulling. The length of your pull depends on the group and how strong you are. Often strong riders stay at the front for longer turns to get a better or harder spin while the weaker ones although they are in the draft still have to work hard to keep up. It evens out differences in ability and means a mixed group can still ride together at a similar effort. So the stronger riders doing the hard work are at the front, while the weaker ones are having to work just as hard to stay on their wheels. Every so often the rider on the outside line rolls through. He accelerates slightly until he is past the rider on the inside then he pulls over. The rider who was behind him rolls through and up onto the front beside him. I started near the back of the group and was getting plenty of shelter from the wind. We were going a lot faster than I would on a solo ride but because everyone is sharing the work the pace on group rides is usually faster than when you ride alone. Due to the fact that you're in the draft for long periods you can sustain the higher speeds.

So we're rolling along and like I said I started near the back, but as the lines rotate I'm moving closer to the front and closer to having to take my 'pull'. I'm getting more and more nervous the closer I get to the front because I'm already working hard just to keep up and I know that the effort level will spike as soon as I have to ride in the wind. Suddenly I'm at the front and the effort does jump very quickly. I start to panic a little bit. There's no way I'm going to be able to sustain this and I'm going to look weak and slow the group down and I'm going to look stupid for trying to ride with these guys. But while I'm busy panicking a strange thing happens. Now I call it 'settling', but then I didn't know how to describe what was happening. The speed stays the same and the effort is much higher than when I was in the group. It's higher than I thought I could sustain, but my body starts to adjust to the new workload. I realise that it's alright – I can do this, so I stop panicking. I'm certainly not able to hold a conversation with the rider beside me. My answers to his conversation aren't much more than grunts because I'm breathing too hard to string any words together but I'm amazed to discover that although it is hard and it hurts it also feels good. My breathing is fast, my legs are buzzing with the effort and my heart is thumping in my chest but it feels really good. I start to feel strong and confident. I'm sitting up here in the wind riding hard and getting this big buzz from the endorphins or adrenaline or whatever . . . and I'm loving it.

Then I learn about something new. It's called 'half wheeling'. Cycling has lots of unspoken rules and unusual etiquette and half wheeling is frowned upon in group riding. When you're on the front you're supposed to sit with your front wheel in line with the guy beside you. Not six inches ahead, because if you do that it can cause issues. The rider beside me thinks he's going too slow and speeds up. I see him coming up alongside and speed up causing him to accelerate again and all of a sudden the pace is too high. I start to drift back and something has happened to that incredibly strong, slightly invincible 'I could pull up here all day' feeling I had only ninety seconds ago.

That wonderful feeling is gone, only to be replaced by a horrible burning build-up of lactic acid in my legs and despite the brain screaming at the legs to push they have decided they are taking no further part in this game. I now suffer the humiliation of getting dropped off the front. I look over my left shoulder hoping the second rider will let me pull in. He nods and opens a gap. I move in and give one last effort to hold the wheel in front of me trying desperately not to get dropped completely. I'm absolutely on my limit just to stay here. Slowly, very slowly, I recover and after a while I'm able to grunt replies again to the other rider's conversations as the group continues to rotate. It's amazing how quickly you learn a lesson from a good kicking. It's just as amazing how quickly you forget that lesson and go back for more. But not today, because today I'm glad just to survive in the group and return home with them.

That winter I learned what it meant to ride in all conditions, including rain, hail, sleet and snow. And for the most part I enjoyed it, even the very hard ones. Something I read about back then has stuck with me ever since: 'Even a hard, cold, wet day on the bike is better than a good day in work.' I still sometimes have to repeat that over and over to myself now on the really miserable, freezing days to stop myself from turning back early.

The first time I ever rode in the snow I was out with the racing group and by now was becoming more familiar with a lot of the group riding etiquette and had learned not to half wheel and to call the holes in the road so the rider behind would know what was coming as all he could see was my backside. About ninety minutes into the ride it started to snow. At that point we were about as far from home as we were going to get, as the ride was planned to be about three hours. Already my hands and feet were numb and sore with the cold but it was out of the question to complain. We like to think we're hard men, despite our skinny or maybe even scrawny, Lycra clad appearance. There's a whole lot of ego and testosterone floating around a club training ride. Despite or maybe because of the suffering, there was a building sense not quite of pleasure, but of satisfaction. We were doing something that most other people would consider nuts, riding for hours in the middle of winter in a snowstorm. This was really hard and I was doing it alongside these guys that I looked up to and admired. I aspired to become what they were.

I became aware of every sensation, like my hot breath being snatched by the wind but warming my chin before it passed. I could feel the heat of my body from the effort and the sweat building slowly to dampen my clothing, while at the same time I could hardly move my fingers to change gears or brake. My legs were feeling that sweet buzz of the effort of the work but at a level that I could sustain for a long time. The cold spreading momentarily through my insides as I take a slug of my freezing cold drink. Then the rise of effort and the feeling of strength as I took a turn on the front pulling into the wind and driving snow. By now I knew how to ride level and hold the group at the same pace. My body adjusted to the extra work and settled into the new rhythm, one that I could sustain but maybe just not for as long. There was no conversation, or very little. We were all inside our own heads, some feeling good and taking some sort of perverse pleasure in the suffering, while for others there was no pleasure in it, perverse or not, but only the suffering. Often I switched from one to the other and back again several times during the ride. One minute I was struggling, wishing I was anywhere except on this damn bike, the next I was back in the zone. All systems were cruising.

Then the rider beside me signalled for me to roll through. He'd had enough on the front and wanted a break. We rotated through and I was still feeling good. At some stage during the ride I realised that for the first time since I'd been on these group rides I was taking full turns at the front and I didn't always feel like I was at my limit. That gave me a real buzz inside. I felt like I was becoming a cyclist.

I got home after the ride and I could hardly stand to walk on feet that were so cold and sore and numb. But the first thing I did before going inside to get warm, clean, dry and fed was to go out the back of the house and hose down my bike. Like I said, there are rules and etiquette. You never leave your bike dirty after a ride. When I had done that it took me ages to strip off my sodden filthy kit at the back door because my fingers wouldn't work. I got into the shower and the heat was heavenly. Heavenly that was until the horrible, painful pins and needles of returning circulation in my hands and feet started. I didn't even wash. I just stood there eyes closed, head under the spray, hot water running off me in dirty little salty rivulets for ages before I start to scrub off. I dressed and ate and then headed into work feeling a little bit epic. I'd done something special today. Something hard that I've never done before and I've started to learn just a little about how to suffer.

By then I had joined a road cycling club and trained almost all the time in my club kit. It gave me a really strong sense of identity. In my head I had at the same time the conflicting feelings of both fitting in and standing out. For the first time in my life I was a member of a club, and not just any club, a cycle racing club. Cycling is very much a minority sport and road racing is an even smaller minority of cyclists. I felt different and somehow special as a result. I hadn't even pinned a number on my back at that stage and my first race was still months away, but I was taking steps and changing myself from who I had been into someone else and I was loving the transformation.

Days turned into weeks, winter into spring and before I knew it my first road race was upon me. I was terrified, because I had no idea what to expect when I showed up. I parked, took out the bike and checked it over. Then I got into my kit and just did what everyone else seemed to be doing. I got on and pedalled up and down warming up and waiting for the start. I recognised a couple of guys from the shop but was too nervous to get into conversation so I nodded a greeting and kept on spinning the legs. I had no idea if I'd done enough training to be here but there was nothing to be done about that now. We lined up at the start, filling the full width of the road and listened to what was to become the familiar warnings about racing on open roads, obeying the laws and not crossing the white line.

It was a handicapped race meaning that the third category riders, veterans (vets) and juniors started first. The second cats a couple of minutes later and the really impressive and very intimidating looking first cats last. The idea was that if the handicap system was done right all the groups would come together somewhere close to the finish.

We were started and the shock to the system was instant. There was no gentle build into a pace. The juniors, who didn't seem to need any time to warm up, were on the front driving hard. There was jostling for place as the group tried to sort itself out. I hadn't ridden in such a big group and never this hard from the gun. I'll never keep this up I thought, panicking. I didn't dare go near the front. I knew what my limit was and was hanging on for dear life and not getting dropped. Then I settled, the body gradually accepting that this was what was going on and it decided to cooperate. I'm not saying I was comfortable or ready to take a turn on the front. I just wasn't feeling like I was going to vomit. I breathed a sigh of relief and thought 'Ok Robbo, make yourself small, hide from the wind and stay in the draft in the middle of the bunch. No heroics and nothing stupid and you might survive this.' I couldn't believe that there were conversations going on around me. Where the hell were they getting the extra oxygen to do that?

It was just about that time that the bunch changed shape. A road race is fluid and always moving, morphing and you've got to be constantly watching what's happening so you don't get caught out – that is if you have any idea what you're looking for, and I certainly didn't.

All I noticed was that the older looking riders, the super lean ones, all popping veins, muscles, rippling calves and bulging quads, looking like they'd been carved from stone, were now moving up to the front. It seems that most of the older guys take a little bit longer to get warmed up but when they get their engines up to speed it's like they've all had turbo chargers added.

The pace went up a notch and things got louder. The vets, who like to shout loudest, wanted to get as many as possible sharing the workload and keeping away for as long as possible from the chasing cat 1 and cat 2 riders who were hunting us down. They were also fairly vocal about letting you know what they thought about 'wheel suckers', someone who wouldn't contribute to the speed but was happy to benefit from everyone else's work. I was constantly hearing shouts of 'ride through, hold the wheel and take a turn', usually accompanied by some choice expletives. I was new and inexperienced and I didn't know if it was aimed at me or just the way all races went, being random shouts of abuse the whole time but I felt like a shirker and a waster and didn't want to look lazy.

I then pulled out into the right-hand line that was rolling through to take a turn in the wind. We were riding fast and I hit the front panicking a bit at the speed but the turns were short and almost immediately the next rider rolled over and in front of me. I recovered as I drifted back into the bunch. Buoyed by the fact that I'd survived my turn on the front I pulled out into the right-hand line again and again I rolled through and back into the group my effort higher this time, but I was too busy being all proud of myself to notice. The third time I rolled through my legs started to fill with lactate and all of a sudden I was on my limit. In fact I was over it and struggling to hold the wheel in front as I drifted back into the bunch. My breathing was coming in hard ragged gasps. My legs were full and burning and I just couldn't turn the pedals fast enough and when riders stopped coming past me I glanced back to realise I was the last man and was losing the bunch. The gap was about two bike lengths. I rose out of the saddle and sprinted to get back on pushing myself way back into the red again. I got back to the last wheel, legs and lungs burning and my heart feeling like it would burst through my chest and just hung on for dear life. I knew if I was dropped it would be a long slow ride home. The pace eased suddenly and I almost ran into the rider in front. Moving out and around him I managed to work my way back into the middle of the group and hide from the wind and recover.

Happy now to ignore the shouts to take a turn, I hid, making myself as small as possible, while trying to avoid every last bit of the wind. Gradually I recovered and after a while I thought that I would make it to the finish as long as I didn't do anything else stupid.

Then the chasing group of cat 1 and 2 riders arrived and they rode straight up the outside like a freight train. Roars of 'Up,Up,Up' from the vets warned that they were coming through. I looked over in awe at the power and speed of the riders driving it but the penny still hadn't dropped. I still hadn't realised what was coming. Maybe the lactic acid had seeped into my brain and affected it or something. Then they get to the front and our group reacted, accelerated and attached itself onto the train and very quickly I'm on my limit again. I start to drift back through the bunch thinking I'll be riding in alone and I'll suffer the indignity and humiliation of being dropped. Then just as suddenly as it ramped up, the gas was off and they all sat up.

I nearly ran into the wheel in front again before I react. I still had no clue as to what was going on. Then I heard conversations start. It was over. That was the finish line and I was so focused on the wheel in front and not getting shelled out the back that I didn't even see it. I'd made it around without getting dropped. On the cool down I chatted to some of the guys I recognised and we swapped our stories of the race before packing up and heading home, sore but very satisfied.

I was out riding later in the week with one of the vets I'd got to know fairly well and we had become good friends. He had almost thirty years riding in his legs, most of that time spent racing. He had raced as a cat 1 at a national level and did well, winning a handful of races along the way but never took the step to race in Europe and never seriously considered turning professional.

We were talking about the race and our very different perspectives of it. The only similarities in our experience was that we both got a huge buzz from it. I recounted how much harder it was than I'd expected it to be and that I couldn't imagine it ever getting easier. I told him I couldn't believe that there were guys strong and fit enough to be able to chat in the bunch while racing at that speed, while I couldn't even let go of the bars long enough to wipe the spit, snot and streaming tears from my face. He assured me it would get easier and even told me that within a couple of races I'd be doing the same, sitting in and chatting. I had come to trust his advice but I was far from convinced. However, it eventually turned out that he was right.

That season was spent doing mostly inter-club racing after work, with the occasional open race at the weekend as the shop allowed. The open races tended to be bigger fields that were longer and faster, whereas the club racing I did was restricted to five local clubs. The club races involved smaller numbers and ran once a week in the evenings after work. The speed might have been a little slower than the open races but there were less places to hide which meant you worked almost as hard.

The club league had a number of benefits for me. I raced every week so I learned how to race effectively very quickly. I suppose I had to learn how to race smart, because I didn't have the big engine to just ride off the front in a breakaway or the massive acceleration needed to be up there in a sprint. I learned who to watch and what to look out for as a race progressed. My bike handling became better and my fitness, speed and strength all saw a big improvement that year.

During my first season I had a couple of top ten finishes but was nowhere close to a win. The gradual improvement through the season kept me motivated and I went hard at winter training again in the off season.

My second season was really just a gradual build on the first, until we did a club race on a circuit that I hadn't ridden before. It was a one-lap race on a very hilly course. It started off exactly the same as every other race – fast from the gun, knowing the second and third group were chasing hard. The first third of the circuit was on roads I knew well and rode regularly. It was mostly flat or gently rolling and dragging but there were no real climbs. So far all of the races I'd done were on similar terrain. I had learned to stay right up at the front of the bunch as much as possible. Although you had less shelter and more time in the wind it was safer there.

At this stage I wasn't under too much pressure, taking turns on the front so I was happy with the trade off. It's also the best place to be in order to react to an attack (not that I had either the legs or knowledge to spot or react to one at that stage). If you're sitting down the back of the group and someone with a good chance of staying away attacks you're too far away from the action to react.

We turned off the main road and we hit the first short hill and almost immediately I moved up from about the third row to the front without either trying or intending to do so. More than a little surprised at myself, I eased off. I didn't want to go shooting off the front only to be caught two minutes later, getting spat out the back. I wasn't familiar with this part of the circuit so I didn't know how long the climb was. All the way up the short climb I was trying to figure out why everyone was going so easy. We crested and I moved back into the group on the descent. The road rolled for a while before dropping sharply into a small valley with a steep climb out of it. Again as soon as the road tipped up I had to back right off so as not to go off the front. I couldn't figure out what was going on, why the race was so slow. Just at that moment came the familiar shouts signifying the arrival of the first and second cat riders. Their group was small, whittled down to five riders and they just rode straight through and off the front.

But still nothing happened. Nobody reacted and the gap was opening. I didn't wait any longer and jumped without really thinking it through. Within a couple of seconds I was up with them. I wasn't cruising now. I was working hard but was still fairly comfortable. I also wasn't hanging on the last wheel but comfortably moving up the outside and slotted in behind the lead rider. He glanced over and did a quick double take, wondering who the hell this toolbox was. He gave a tiny nod and then he looked away. I felt like I was going to explode with excitement. I was climbing with the fast guys and they weren't dropping me. In fact a quick glance over my shoulder made me realise that I was the only one who had bridged over. I checked again, there were five others. I was in the points even if I finished last and would win my category for the first time. Something about counting chickens before hatching should probably have come to mind. But I felt incredible and I was dancing on the pedals. I'd never had a day like this on the bike before. It felt so easy I thought, as I was practically giddy with the excitement. We crested and started a fast, twisty descent and I suddenly realised that there was more to staying with a bunch of first and second cats than just having good climbing legs.

I was immediately last and getting dropped. I pushed hard and tried to follow their lines into corners. I was way out of my depth and almost crashed twice on the tight twisty descent. I couldn't believe I was getting dropped on the way down after staying with them so easily on the climb. I was off the back. The last rider disappeared around the corner ahead and

I just kept going as fast as I dared to the bottom, at which point it went straight back up again.

This next section of the race was all up and down. Climb, twisty descent, another climb then another twisty descent. I hit the bottom of the next rise as hard as I could and rode full gas into it. I still felt incredibly strong, stronger than I'd ever felt before. I caught them about half way up and tried to settle and recover, but there was no chance of that on a hill. Again we crested and again I got dropped on the way down but not as badly this time. The next climb started immediately again and I rose out of the saddle and accelerated but this time the kick wasn't there. I was working so hard to get back on after the descents I wasn't able to recover for another effort. I sat back down almost accepting that was it . . . game over.

I tried once more and got back up out of the saddle, head screaming at the legs to just push once more. This was the last climb and descent and the next ten kilometres had enough flat to recover. 'You will recover, just stay on the wheels, just hang on', I told myself. I managed to latch on just at the crest of the hill. On the last technical descent though they opened a gap. Only a bike length but I was out of the draft and my legs were fried. I dug as deep as I could just once more and got back on. Then they accelerated for no particular reason, just someone feeling good, so he hit the gas a little bit and that finished me. I blew up completely. One minute I was hanging on the tail of the group at 50kph thinking I'm home and dry, but the next I was hardly able to push the pedals at 25kph.

I was gutted, and to make matters worse I was going to get caught any second now and get dropped straight out of the main bunch because my legs were so fried. But they didn't arrive and my legs gradually cleared and my breathing came under control. I started to push again waiting for the bunch to catch me but another two kilometres went by and there was no sign of them. My legs were almost back when they finally caught me with less than five kilometres to go.

I got out of the saddle to accelerate back up to the speed of the bunch and sat in for a couple of minutes. As we got near the end I decided that

I was going to go for the sprint, but from a long way out. I don't like the craziness of a big bunch sprint in the last 200-300mts.

Maybe the legs were still there and just maybe I could get that point and category win. I moved up through the bunch. The tension rises in the last couple of kilometres as everyone is watching and waiting and jostling for position.

It was way too early when I attacked. There was almost a kilometre to go but I went anyway – as hard as I could. Two guys reacted instantly. I pushed again and nosed in front and they both came alongside me. We were three abreast and I could see the finish line coming up fast. I went one more time, giving it all I had and I got half a bike length then a bit more and then it was over.

I've never worked so hard for a sixth place finish before or since. I could hardly stand when I got off the bike. My legs were wobbly and really sore, but it was the best feeling I'd ever had in a race.

CHAPTER 5
HOOKED ON IRON

The first thing I did before I even got out of bed was to reach for a cigarette. My head was pounding and every movement sent a fresh wave of pain jolting through my skull. My stomach was very sick just lying still, so moving wasn't even an option yet, except to reach over for my cigarettes of course.

I slept with water beside the bed. My mouth always felt like someone had emptied a stinking vacuum bag into it during the night. It was dry, with a stinking breath and tasted rank. One of the really unpleasant side effects of being a heavy smoker was made worse this morning by the presence of a thundering hangover.

I made my way downstairs slowly, trying not to make either the pain or nausea worse. I made a strong coffee and planted myself in front of the television where I fully intended to spend most of that Sunday. I had no idea that I was going to begin a journey that would change everything about me – who I was and my way of life. It wasn't a change that became visible for years but this day was the spark that started it.

I flicked through my usual selection of sports and news channels, settling on Eurosport. There was some sort of bike race on. I was only half watching to be honest until I thought I heard a description of what they were doing. Something about swimming first then biking and then running, but what really stopped me in my tracks were the distances. I thought he said they were going to get off the bike and run a marathon. Surely that couldn't be right?

I didn't know much about athletics, cycling or swimming and had never even heard of this sport called Ironman triathlon, that mixed all three, but I did know that a marathon was long, really long, and I believed it was almost impossible for most ordinary people to do just that on its own, never mind after tortuous periods of swimming and biking.

These people were as far away from my reality as Michael Schumacher. They all looked incredibly fit, muscular, strong and tanned. They were obviously all blessed with some sort of super gene or natural talent, they weren't normal I thought. They looked like they were from a different planet. They had my attention and I started listening to the commentators talking about how the race was unfolding, but I really only wanted to hear that bit again about the distances, because I must have been mistaken.

Then they said it again. You know the way commentators have to fill time during a long race? Well this one was certainly long. The swim was 2.4 miles, the bike race was 112 miles and the run was a full marathon 26.2 miles. I still hadn't figured things out. How many days do they have to do this, I wondered?

The athletes looked incredible. I couldn't get over how perfect they looked. They had this absolutely aspirational physique, with wide muscular shoulders and strong arms. Their wide backs tapered down to a slim waist and they had very ripped legs. And they were all bronzed and glistening with sweat while they baked under the Hawaiian sun. Then they talked about the distances again and this time my hungover brain took in the information. They do them one after the other without stopping. I was dumbstruck. I thought it was the coolest thing I'd ever heard of. Cool and unbelievably crazy.

I was wide awake now and on to my second coffee and paying full attention. There seemed to be a couple of strange things going on though. There was more than one race. There were the professionals, which did not surprise me, as I had assumed that anyone fit enough to do this sort of crazy race must be a professional sports person. But they were also talking about 'age groupers'. I'd no idea who these were at first, but it became clear that they were amateurs. This was the world championship for both professionals and amateurs and they all raced together. It must be cool to get to start alongside the best in the world I thought. You couldn't get out there and race with Michael Schumacher or toss a ball around with Michael Jordan.

Then they cut to a guy still in the swim. I couldn't really figure out what was going on. He was coming to the end of the swim and had a harness around his torso attached to a rope, pulling along a small dinghy. Inside it was a man lying twisted and contorted. The commentator said they were a father and son called Rick and Dick Hoyt. Dick, the father was swimming. Rick the grown up son, a quadriplegic with cerebral palsy was in the dinghy. Dick reached the point where he could stand and dragged the dinghy over, took off the harness and reached in and lifted his grown up son into his arms, the way you carry a toddler up to bed out in front of you lying draped across both arms. He then walked up the steps onto the pier surrounded by crowds cheering, clapping and some actually crying.

I'd never seen anything like it. I was moved to the point that I had to take a deep breath and compose myself. I wasn't going to start crying. Dick half ran, half walked carrying his son to their bike. It was a custom built one and looked like a cross between a tandem and a bike with a child seat but out in front not behind. Dick carefully placed Rick into the seat, fastened his harness put on both their helmets then started towards the start of the bike course.

Just like that I was immediately hooked. It cut back and forward from the bike course and the professionals to age groupers they were following through the race, usually ones with a story, like someone who had survived a disease or accident and somehow managed to get themselves to what they called The Ironman and back again to Rick and Dick.

At some point during the coverage I went from thinking this is the craziest thing I've ever seen to this is the coolest thing I've ever seen. From there I somehow ended up thinking I was going to do that. I had no idea what that meant at the time, but I just knew it was something I promised to myself I would do.

Here I was hung over, sick, unfit and almost chain smoking, thinking I could someday race with these incredible people. The pros continued on to the marathon but they were as far away from my reality as the planet Mars. The age group stories were fascinating and motivating but these people, like the pros were obviously genetic freaks or gifted or had some massive God-given talent. They had overcome some huge obstacle to get themselves here and that made their story incredible.

Watching Dick on the bike doing something in so many ways harder than what the pros or age groupers were doing, while at the same time looking like an ordinary person was amazing. He was an ordinary person not just doing what looked like an impossible event, but doing it in such a way as to make the seemingly impossible even harder. I saw him as an ordinary person. Obviously Dick is one of the most incredible people not just in the world of triathlon but in any walk of life. The more of his story that the commentators told, about his life as a lieutenant colonel in the Air National Guard and how they first started in a five-mile running race coming second last, to here with the best of the best in the world at The Ironman. The more I saw him as a real person, the more I saw him as someone I could identify with. He didn't start out as a super hero but through bloody mindedness, love for his son and hard work he was here. That seemed to me then like proof that it could be done.

I don't remember any other details from that race. I forgot who won and I couldn't even name one of the pros but Rick and Dick changed something in me that day. I watched the race unfold still amazed and fascinated at every part of it but I was captivated by the Hoyts' story. They were on to the marathon but Dick was reduced to periods of walking because of exhaustion, but he still kept going. The sun went down and whenever the camera came back to them they were still going, never for a second giving up. Dick was slowing so much though that he wasn't going to make the cut-off time. The race had an allotted time and if you didn't finish inside that you didn't finish.

I was willing him on, sitting on the edge of my seat almost shouting at the television. Knowing he wasn't going to make it in time, and that the race was over made no difference. He kept on moving, running when he could, walking when he had to. It was the most impressive feat I'd ever seen a 'normal' person do. He didn't make the cut-off. He was still out on the course when they stopped the clock and shut off the lights. The finish chute and arch on Ali'i Drive went dark, but he still didn't stop.

The camera bike with him was obviously able to relay his position back to the organisers and they weren't giving up on him. He mightn't get an official finish but they could still welcome him in. The crowds stayed, or maybe word spread that he was nearly home. At the finish line there's a long chute the competing athletes run in that earlier had been lined five and six deep with spectators, but had since emptied. Long after the race was over it was full again, as people came back to witness and welcome them and as the Hoyts ran down the chute, the spotlights came back on. Dick had tears running down his face, as did a lot of the spectators and race staff. I was fighting hard with the lump in my throat.

My Ironman journey had begun, or rather the seed had been planted. But life has a habit of getting in the way and it would be another seven or eight years before I came across Rick and Dick Hoyt again and that seed started to grow.

CHAPTER 6
LOSING MY TRIATHLON VIRGINITY - DUBLIN CITY TRIATHLON 2003

I looked over my shoulder exiting the water. There were only a handful of people behind me. I ran into transition, glad to have survived the swim and really looking forward to the next part. I'd had a couple of seasons of road racing and although I hadn't raced that year my biking was probably what you would call decent, compared to my swimming. I came 155th out of 161 out of the water and I'd done the whole thing breaststroke because I couldn't swim front crawl.

As soon as I was out of transition I immediately started catching and passing people on the bike, making up almost 100 places, moving up into the top fifty. Then came the run and my running though not quite as bad as the swim wasn't far off it. I went on to be re-passed by about seventy of the people I'd caught on the bike to finish 117th in a time of 2:52:54 for my first Olympic distance race. This was my first triathlon.

Unlike any road race I'd done before there were people still there, cheering and congratulating me for finishing, in 117th place in the bike race. They was still a crowd there for the last person to cross the line. I'd been dropped once from the bunch in my last road race about ten kilometres from the end and rolled in probably only five minutes down and almost everyone was already gone home, including the guy that I'd given my backpack to put in his car. In the backpack were my house keys, wallet and phone. I cycled the twenty-five kilometres home and spent the next two hours shivering and starving, sitting in the shed, waiting to get into the house.

I was dropped because I hadn't been training hard enough and was only dipping in and out of racing. I wasn't fit enough and it was a bad enough experience to put me off going back for a while. That's a big part of why I decided to try triathlon, and judging by the welcome at the end, post-race food and how friendly and approachable everyone was it was the right choice. I loved it and got such a huge kick out of the whole event I knew I'd be back for more.

That was near the end of the 2003 season and I'd fully intended to learn how to swim properly over the winter and race the next season but I'd lost the desire and drive.

I became lazy and before I fully realised it, 2004 was gone. I kept on making excuses when customers asked if I was racing and I hated doing that. I hated being the guy who always has a good reason why he couldn't get things done. . . why he didn't train and wasn't fit. The only reason I didn't do it was that I didn't decide it was important enough to make time for it.

Winter 2004 came and I finally found the drive and motivation to start training again. Despite getting swimming lessons I still couldn't master the front crawl and spent most of my training doing the breaststroke. At the time I was still a complete beginner and all of my sessions were short, but I was fairly consistent and went to my first (pool-based) race of that year – 2005 – in what I thought was better shape.

During April in Ireland the water is too cold to swim outdoors. I finished the race mid-pack and loved it. This time the hook was well and truly in and I went into work the following Monday and went through the entire race calendar, selected the races I wanted to join and printed the entry forms. I filled them in and posted them off with a cheque for my entry fee.

It was still old-school printed entry forms, cheques, envelopes and licking stamps. It's incredible to think that that process has changed so much now with online entry and big races selling out thousands of places in minutes. In only eight or nine years paper entry is almost extinct.

The year 2005 was another of those major tipping points for me. I raced twelve triathlons from sprint to half Ironman. I went back bike racing, raced half a dozen duathlons and rode a number of 100 and 200k sportive events. I was fitter than I'd ever been, but I was still very much a newbie triathlete. In fact I didn't even think of myself as a triathlete – more like a cyclist who did a couple of triathlons. I joined a triathlon club and immersed myself in the whole lifestyle of training and racing and spent every spare minute learning and reading about races, bikes, bike fitting and anything else I could get my hands on.

Again the business followed my passion and the bike shop gradually became more and more specialist. The business grew as I catered more for triathletes, as the word spread and as I was seen at more races.

I ended the season completing my first half Ironman. It's one of Ireland's most iconic races, called 'The Lost Sheep' and is held in the south County Kerry town of Kenmare. I had no idea how to train for it and really hoped that one fifteen-kilometre run would suffice, on top of my Olympic distance racing and normal training. I was starting to feel like a bit of a legend by the end of the season as I had racked up a whole season of triathlon and bike racing and was improving all the time, admittedly from a very low starting point. I was now usually in the top third and occasionally even cracked the top thirty in races. Even so, I was about to learn a very hard lesson. I'm sure there is some expression that fits my situation then – 'pride before a fall' or some expression like that?

Anyway, the week leading into the race probably typified not just my slightly over-the-top personality but also my misguided but growing feelings of invincibility. The previous Saturday saw me race an Olympic distance triathlon. The next day, Sunday, I did a 100km bike event. Three days later, on Wednesday, I did a local duathlon. This is probably not what you'd call an ideal taper week for a half Ironman, and certainly the furthest thing from clever for a first-year newbie. Race day arrived and I was nervous at the start, but also really excited. I had it figured out that a half Ironman distance is well suited to a strong biker and I thought that I'd do well. But this was stupid and naive. The swim was also sufficiently short in relation to the other two, so I thought I wouldn't loose as much time when looking at the overall race.

It was grey and the water was choppy and we were told there were currents, and to be careful with our sighting in order to stay on course. The only advantage of breast- stroking the whole race was I was fairly certain to go in a straight line. I exited the water in the middle of the field, surprising not just myself but any of the supporters there who knew how bad a swimmer I was.

I was delighted with this outcome and wasted no time getting on the bike course to start chasing people down. The course seemed to suit me, having a mountain in the middle of it, and sure enough I spent the next hour gradually moving up the field. We went over the climb and down one of the most technical descents I've ever raced and onto the next rolling section. I was feeling great, eating and drinking and still making my way up the field. Then I felt a sharp pain at the back of the knee and immediately slowed right down. I couldn't pedal at all without bad pain, but I still had a long way to go to get back. Even worse than the pain at this point was the humiliation of being re-passed by all of the people I'd gone by. I guessed they thought I just blew up and didn't know how to pace myself, but I felt stupid, angry and gutted.

I arrived back to transition and smiled and waved to my family as I limped through, racked my bike and tried gingerly to start the run. The pain wasn't getting any worse and I thought I would just run easy, as I really badly wanted to finish.

Within one kilometre I was alternating walking with short 300-400-metre runs. By the four- kilometre mark I was reduced to a fast walk, and the pain was getting worse all the time. The back of my knee exploded with pain every time I took a step. The run course is one of the hilliest in any race in Ireland and is famous for its difficulty. Soon I was reduced to a shuffling limping walk and had to keep stopping to let the pain subside enough to continue. I walked past the ambulance a couple of times and was offered a lift back when they saw me walking and limping so badly only a couple of kilometres into a half marathon. I refused and told them I was fine.

I kept going and the further I went and the worse the pain got and the harder it became the more I wanted to finish. I was almost last by now and the end of the race kept getting further away instead of closer as I slowed more and more.

I took longer to do the run than the bike race, but I eventually came around the corner to see there was still people waiting for me to finish. They were cheering and shouting at me to run the last twenty metres, which I tried,and I crossed the line to be greeted by my family and friends.

I had tears in my eyes and a feeling inside like nothing else I'd ever experienced. I didn't want to suppress it or control it. I wanted to go on feeling this massive rush of emotion and satisfaction. I never wanted to forget this feeling.

At that time I had done something that I didn't think was possible for me and it didn't matter that I'd come in last. I had learnt more about myself with my worst race performance in the hardest conditions than I'd learnt in all the races I'd participated in during the last five years.

I felt stronger in a different way, not physically, but mentally and emotionally. That race was one of the pivotal points in my life, when I realised that one can stretch one's perceived limits away further than one could believe.

I saw a physiotherapist the next week and she told me I'd torn both the calf and hamstring at the point where they join the knee. She reckoned they happened one at a time. In other words, I had done the second injury during my walk to the finish.

I'm not sure that I should admit it, but that made me perversely proud. I think it reinforced the realisation that I could push myself that much further than I could ever have thought.

CHAPTER 7
LEARNING TO SWIM –
WINTER 2005

I finished 2005 injured after the Lost Sheep Half Ironman, widely recognised as being one of the hardest races in the country. It is held in Kenmare in the south west of Ireland at the end of the season each year. I was also hugely motivated for the following season. I had orders from the physiotherapist not to run for six weeks but I was allowed to swim and in two or three weeks I could get back on the bike for short easy spins straight away.

I decided that I would do what I could, so for the next six weeks I swam four or five mornings and two or three evenings, although 'swim' wasn't quite the right word at that point.

I'd been given a DVD with a swim system that would take me from not being able to swim to swimming in less than six weeks. The system was called Total Immersion and it broke the total stroke down into small parts that could be mastered one at a time.

The problem with learning to swim is that there is a lot going on all at once and at the same time you have the ever-present risk of death from drowning. Your right hand is doing something different to your left, your body should be rotating, your legs kicking but not from the knee. You kick from the hip. I didn't even know there was a difference, and I certainly couldn't tell which I was doing. I just knew it wasn't working for me. All I knew for certain was that if I only kicked I didn't move. I lay there stretched out holding on to a kick board kicking up a mini tsunami behind me – but there was no movement. Add in the fact that you can only breathe when you remember to remove your face from the water and it's a hell of a steep learning curve. My problem is that I'm not a particularly well-coordinated individual. I'm not clumsy, well not really. But what my head thinks is going on is often very different to the actual reality of my body's movement.

So back to this swimming lark. Total Immersion had the stroke broken down into a couple of dozen drills and that suited me because I only needed to concern myself with two things at a time to begin – the drill itself and not breathing in while face down in the water.

Good plan, sounds simple? Not quite so!

I drank a lot of pool water for the first couple of weeks. Chlorine might be great for pool hygiene but it is not as tasty as you might think.

I'd show up with fins or a pull buoy or whatever was needed for each particular drill and spent an hour every day just learning one tiny part of the stroke at a time. As in most busy pools that time of the morning was busy with swim squads, masters' groups, triathletes and people in for their pre-work swim. The pool was set out in lanes and each lane was either reserved for a club or group or had a speed allocation, fast, medium or slow.

Every morning I went straight for the slowest lane. Doing drills means moving slower than if you're actually swimming. Doing the most basic, learning how to build a stroke drill meant I was moving really slowly, even slower than the slowest breast-stroking 75-year-old – not to mention the fact that you look like a complete toolbox.

Each day I'd get up early enough to watch the day's drill before going to the pool, often watching it several times before going, so I knew it by heart. I would then go to the pool and spend the whole hour doing just that drill.

I felt incredibly stupid. I was in a pool full of good swimmers. People at the pool that early tend to be real swimmers and here I was doing this drill where I lay on my side one arm out in front and one down by my side kicking up and down the pool turning my head up to breathe every few seconds.

Let me paint you a picture. Imagine Superman flying along looking strong and cool and fast. Now take away the strong and cool and fast and the cape and the cool blue suit but leave the red speedos then take away all the muscles and you're getting the picture. What's left is a skinny triathlete in his speedos who can't swim and swallows a lot of the pool water.

No one else was doing anything else like it and I felt like a complete clown. I imagined the lifeguards and staff were all wondering what the nut job was up to in the slow lane, but I stuck with it.

I think I did the first drill for three days solid, before moving on to the second one. The instructions were not to attempt the next step until you had the first one perfect. It looked like I was going to be a slow learner. Luckily I had started about six months before my first race.

When I finally mastered the Superman-looking drill I repeated the process with the second one. I watched and learned the day's drill before leaving and driving to the pool in the dark. I headed straight to the slowest lane and did nothing only this one tiny part of the stroke over and over again. The second part of the stroke took maybe two days to learn. The staff all knew me at this stage. They all greeted me and smiled at me like I was a special case, too far gone to help and only to be smiled at and pitied. 'There goes the toolbox again,' they seemed to say.

By the time I was on the third or fourth drill I was managing to master a new one almost daily. As I started to understand the system and how the drills worked they started to "click" faster and I finally felt like I was making progress.

Then one day I woke up, made some coffee and went in to watch the day's lesson. They decided at this stage I was at the end of Section 1 and it was time to add all five bits together at the same time. I nearly choked on my coffee and decided to go back to bed, or into work early or maybe the house needed to be vacuumed? You remember my problem with coordination?

I kicked myself in the backside and watched it over and over until I had it memorised. Then I went to the pool and said hello to the usual suspects and endured the usual pitying looks.

'Poor lad, not much hope for him', they seemed to imply.

I took up my usual place in the slow lane and rehearsed the moves in my head for a minute, then pushed off. The brain knew what to do but none of it happened at all like it was going on in my head. So I had another go but something else was going wrong, distant alarm bells ringing, but I was busy having another try and still having no luck. By now the alarm bells have turned into a full-on red alert and my mind is screaming at me that I need to stop trying to do the stupid move and breathe. Oh yeah.

I stood and gasped and after my breathing had returned to sort of normal, I stopped seeing stars and ascertained that no one saw my ineptness, I have another go.

But it's the same sad result.

Three days of struggle and gallons of heavily chlorinated water later . . . it finally clicks. I can't believe it, but I have succeeded!

Don't get so excited Robbo, I think to myself. That's only part one of six, and each part has a bunch of smaller parts. So I drill up and down, mostly getting it right, and the next day I come back to do it again.

Let's take a quick break from the pool while I tell you a little more about myself. I think at it's both one of my biggest strengths and weaknesses – at the same time. A little like Superman and Kryptonite, one is good for him and one steals all his powers. Don't get me wrong, I'm not comparing myself to Superman. He can shoot lasers out of his eyes and can fly. I obviously can't do either of those things. Apart from that, the comparison should be obvious.

Anyway what I was going to tell you about is what I call my 'blinkers.' As in what you make a horse wear so that it doesn't become distracted. Well I sort of wear a pair of blinkers. First I'll tell you how my mind works, and then I'll get on to the blinkers.

First I look at all the options, whether it's a business decision, training or anything else, including for instance, learning how to swim. I'll examine said options, weigh them all up and then make a decision based on all the information I've got at hand. Once the decision is made the blinkers go on. At that point I've got all the benefits, but at the same time also the dangers of wearing blinkers.

When the blinkers are on they allow me to ignore all other distractions and go after something relentlessly. This can be a huge strength because I put all of my energy only into looking and constantly heading in the direction of my target. I stop worrying about risks or what could go wrong. When I decide this is the right course of action I know the risks and accept them. So I think, why worry about them now that I'm committed ? It only uses energy needlessly.

The downside is that I can become a little blinded to any other way of reaching my goal, possibly ending up doing things the hardest way. I possibly don't always realise this as quickly if I made the wrong choice to start with. It's a case of head down, plough on. Every so, I'll often look up to make sure I'm still on course, not realising for a while that I'm heading in the wrong direction. But the end result is that I pretty much always get things done.

Ok, so let's get back to my progress in the pool.

I went back doing the drills and the blinkers were on, indeed had been on for weeks now. I worked my way through all of the individual and combined lessons until one day I reached the end of the DVD and the man said:

'Ok, now you are ready to swim.'

I wasn't so sure, but I thought I'd give it a go. If I had achieved nothing else, at least I'd become absolutely excellent at his drills over the past six weeks.

I got into the pool and swam one length, turned and swam back and I could hardly breathe. I was on my limit just to do two lengths after six weeks of looking like a toolbox doing all of his stupid drills. If he didn't live somewhere on the opposite side of the planet I swore I'd find him and make him eat his damn DVD

I tried again, swimming two more lengths. It was the same result and I had to stop and recover and catch my breath.

I spent a whole hour doing one or two lengths at a time, before having to stop and rest.

I was so angry and disappointed. I was no better than what I had been six weeks ago . . . if anything I was worse off. I was six weeks closer to my race and back where I started, unable to string more than one or two lengths at a time. Admittedly I was actually swimming and probably faster, but that wasn't going to be much use in the sea where there wasn't a wall to hang onto every twenty-five metres, so I could catch my breath.

I went in to work, feeling dejected and gutted. My whole day was spent examining what I could do differently or what I was doing wrong. In the afternoon if it was quiet in the shop and I had all my work done I would often research triathlon equipment, read about races or learn about the new bikes on the market. (You might call it surfing the web, but as I own a triathlon shop, I was justified in calling it research).

That particular day I was consumed with the swim and what had gone wrong. Why hadn't the magic system worked, I kept thinking. To make things worse I stumbled across an article on the internet talking about how important it is to save your legs for the bike and run, so for triathlon you don't really need to kick well, only a little for balance. Besides, the article said, triathlon wetsuits are designed with very buoyant legs, so you don't have to kick to stop your legs sinking, they just float along behind you all on their own.

There's also this little piece of swim equipment called a pull buoy. It's a float that you place between your legs, which stops them from sinking when you don't kick. It's really intended as a way to increase the load on your arms by stopping you from kicking. All the propulsion has to come from your arms, and pull buoys are often used with paddles to make it even harder. Paddles slip on over your hands like little shovels, making it more difficult to pull yourself through the water.

I could see a side street – a way from A to C without going through B. I had come to the conclusion that if I could stop kicking I would reduce how hard I was working and be able to concentrate on just the stroke, which was the most important part.

I couldn't wait to try out this concept. I went to the pool the next morning, headed straight to the equipment room and grabbed a pull buoy. I got into the slow lane and swam six lengths without stopping. I nearly burst with excitement and spent the next hour ploughing up and down in sets of six, eight and ten lengths at a time.

It turned out that my swimming performance was a lot for a beginner. The next day I couldn't lift my arms high enough to scratch my head, but I spent the day grinning like a fool.

I had it. . . I'd finally cracked it. I wasn't quite a swimmer yet and the pull buoy that allowed me to get started sort of turned into a bit of a crutch that took about another two years to wean myself off, but for now it worked.

CHAPTER 8
A MOUNTAIN BIKE RACE

Motivation was high and I was making progress in the pool. I was still using the pull buoy like a crutch. I read more about training and in a very haphazard way started adding in some of the recommendations from magazines, websites and books. It was very much a case of too much information and over-complicating things. But even if it wasn't all exactly the right type of session, I was training fairly regularly and, partly by fluke, getting some of it right.

One of the things that I discovered that year was the difference that 'volume' makes. I was to rediscover this again a couple of years later.

It's a very simple concept – you train more and you get faster. It seems pretty simple, but it's by no means easy. It's not easy because we all have other lives that have nothing to do with triathlon. Relationships, kids, jobs, families, businesses to run and any number of crisis situations that may just arise. Triathlon training for most of us – as much as we don't want to either admit it or like it – may come quite a long way down the list.

I realised that to improve from the last season I would need to train more often and much harder. My swimming was flying. I was having so much fun with it and it was becoming easy to motivate myself to continue to improve. My running ability, after my injury in The Lost Sheep Half Ironman was very slowly returning. But I had never been much of a runner to start with. In order to help in sorting this out and in an effort to combine family life with training, I joined my local running club that had a fantastic kids and junior programme, so I brought my son and daughter along . . . my idea being threefold.

First there was the selfish motivation. I was able to train while at the same time spending time with my kids – sort of. Secondly it meant that my wife was free to do something else other than look after the kids two evenings a week, so it smoothed things at home.

Thirdly, although this might sound corny, was the most important fact that I loved cycling, triathlon and sports and it had opened up a whole new world to me in my late twenties.

I had no illusions that my children would automatically love sport straight away, but I thought that if they do it for a couple of years when they are very young at least they will know about the joys of sport and that they could have it to come back to as teenagers, even if they grow out of it for a while. I wanted them to love sport as much as I did.

I was now running with accomplished athletes and I quickly discovered that a three or four kilometre run wasn't really considered a run at all. It was more like a short warm-up before a 'session', after which they would again do another cool-down run of ten to fifteen minutes. It turned out that was the reason why I never really improved. You actually have to run to become a runner, but I didn't know that at the time I also ran faster than I would run alone. Like I had learned on the bike, training with others pushes you way harder than you will ever do training alone. So over the winter my running also improved for those two basic reasons – quality and volume.

My cycling followed a similar trajectory. I was commuting on my bike as much as possible but had realised that once I reached a certain point, unless it was a hard or quality session an hour wasn't worth a whole lot in terms of training. So I started to double up spins at the weekend. Saturday I headed out early and did a two or three-hour easy ride. Sunday was the club ride, which had enough fast and hard riding to make me see an improvement in my bike performance that had plateaued for a year. Now there was more volume than before, some quality and back-to-back long rides.

In January I was talking to a very good friend of mine about my training and because he was a cycling coach he had a real interest in my progress. He had been giving me tips for a while, so I asked him would he coach me for a couple of months so that at least I knew that if I was putting in all this effort that I was doing the right things.

He agreed, but as he was a bike coach he told me it would be more general on the swim and run and much more specific on the bike part. The first week's programme arrived and I had to start training by heart rate. But first he wanted me to get lactate and Vo2 max testing, so he could set more accurate training zones.

I booked the test with a sports science laboratory and after a couple of weeks headed in for my appointment. They put you on a stationery bike and put on a mask to measure oxygen and CO_2. They also take blood samples at two, three or four-minute intervals depending on the test protocol. All the time you have to increase your power or effort at the same intervals. You keep on going until failure. I've done a couple of them since and I always walk away disappointed, thinking my head gave up before the body, that I gave into the pain too easily.

I don't remember my numbers very well, but I think my Vo2 max was mid to high 60s, which combined with my maximum power output according to the coach would make me a good Category 2 rider or, at a push, a poor Category 1. I was a bit disappointed to discover there wasn't the hidden engine of a Ferrari under the bonnet just waiting to be fine -tuned but I had to work with what I had.

Like the swimming DVD I followed the training plan as closely as I could – life, work and family allowing. I saw two immediate changes, realising it was all either much harder or much easier to become successful. All of what I now call the 'grey area' in the middle was gone. The grey area is the part where you're cruising just a little too hard to hold a comfortable conversation but it's not quite hard enough to be hurt.

I was now working on what I think of as three systems – fitness, strength and speed. Fitness came from the long easy volume, which was easier than I'd been riding or running before. It takes a long time to build, so think several months as opposed to weeks.

Strength came from riding and running hills. But not the way we did on the Sunday club ride, racing to the top out of the saddle and on our limit. No, this was controlled, seated, and in a hard gear at a low cadence. It was like lifting weights but on the bike. I find that this system trains a bit faster and for me has always had a fairly dramatic effect. I usually see improvements in four to six weeks of one or two strength sessions a week.

Speed came from the very high intensity and the short intervals involved. I used to get this naturally from road racing but not in this structured fashion. It's the icing on the cake and it was a small part of the training, but there were small bits of this very high intensity work interspersed with a lot of the sessions as we got close to racing. I often did these on the turbo because it was easier to do maximal efforts safely indoors without running into someone because you were going so hard that you weren't watching where you were going.

The effect of all these changes was very dramatic and all of a sudden I saw big jumps in my fitness level. I was all set to hit the tri season hard, but I had all of this fitness that I couldn't test and I was getting impatient. I decided to go back to have a crack at mountain bike racing again. I entered a race in Castlewellan, up in County Down. I had ridden it a couple of times before and my best placing was in the mid-teens but always miles away from the leaders.

I started by riding a practice lap. I'd been off the mountain bike for about a year and through the twisty technical single-track sections I was very slow, and constantly making mistakes. I was very rusty but confident in my strength and fitness. I could place well here I thought if I didn't do anything stupid at the start.

The course hits a really steep climb after only a couple of hundred metres and I wanted to be in the top ten turning up to the climb. I wasn't going to risk blowing up trying to climb with the leaders, but I didn't want to be too far back either.

The race started hard, as they always do. I managed to hold my place somewhere about tenth, just as we turned onto the big climb. I got out of the saddle and settled into a nice rhythm but I was passing people too quickly. I panicked a bit, thinking I was over-excited and going too hard, so I backed off, but I still moved up another place and another. And it still felt alright. Then the climb flattened out about half-way up for a few metres and rose again.

I was third on the flat section and it still felt really easy. As soon as we turned onto the second half of the climb I threw caution to the wind and hit the gas hard and went off the front. I didn't look back until I turned into the single-track section. I had a decent gap, but this was where I was weakest and sure enough I heard a couple of riders catching up on me. I decided to make myself as wide as possible and ride hard anywhere they could get past and try to recover through the tight twisty sections.

I dropped out onto the next section of the fire road climb, with three riders right behind me and this time I really hit the gas, giving it everything. There was another technical section before the end of the lap and I needed a big lead going in to stay in front. I turned into the forest and tried to get my breathing under control after the climb. I tried to stay smooth and despite the fact that I could hear the other riders coming they didn't quite catch me before the end of the lap. I came through the start finish area in the lead, on my own.

I couldn't believe it, but I still had two laps to go, with three riders chasing hard. I turned onto the big climb at the start of the lap and again went full gas. I needed that lead going into the forest and I wanted this win . . . I could taste it.

I got to the top alone and rode the complete second lap almost solo off the front. I occasionally caught a glimpse of two riders behind as the course looped back and forth through the forest. I rode the second climb the same, as hard as I could and tried to be as smooth as possible through the last technical section, but I was making mistakes on the technical sections as I become tired. Missing my line through rocky sections and over roots and I was having to put my foot down constantly to stabilise myself.

I came through to start the last lap with a slim lead again and hit the bottom of the big climb with all I had. I didn't look back until I was turning into the forest at the top and one of the riders had come after me on the climb and was only twenty metres behind entering the technical section and within seconds he was on my wheel. I slowed right down in the tight sections again to recover and tried to make myself as wide as possible so he couldn't pass where he was stronger. For the last time I dropped out of the forest onto the final climb with him right on my wheel. One more climb, one more technical section and I had it. I hit the last fire road out of the saddle with everything I had and dropped him again. I braked as late as I could and turned down into the last section of forest. He caught me about half way through. There was room for him to pass so I couldn't try to block the trail and I had to ride through this section faster than any other lap, which was way over my limit. Over the small jump and he was almost rubbing my wheel with his. Over the second one and through a difficult off camber switchback and he was still there, but there was only one more section and then a fifty-metre sprint to the finish. Just as I was thinking that I was sure I could take him in a sprint, my face hit the ground! My front wheel wiped out on a wet root I had ridden over a half dozen times that day without a problem. He was so close to me that he could do nothing except ride over me. I'm was on my feet in seconds and did a running mount, but it was too late as he'd got a gap and crossed the line two bike lengths ahead of me.

I was completely gutted, because I couldn't believe I had come so close and lost. I couldn't believe I had lost the way I did. It was my first ever chance at a win and I lost it with fifty metres to go.

It's was by far my best placing in any race, but I never felt worse. I shook the winner's hand smiled and congratulated him. I couldn't face waiting around for the prize giving so I made my excuses to the organiser about having a long drive back and apologized, collected my prize pack and departed.

I now had a hunger for a win and a belief that I could get one. All of a sudden I was competitive in my category. I showed up for the next four races but didn't place higher than third and wasn't in the running for a win in any of them. That first race in Castlewellen in Northern Ireland played right into my strengths and forgave my weaknesses. I was strong and fit, so all the climbing suited me but I wasn't riding the mountain bike enough to improve my technical skills. The following races had less climbing and much more technical single track and I just wasn't able to compete with the good mountain bikers.

I accepted that I couldn't do both triathlon and mountain bike (MTB) properly and despite my newfound enjoyment of getting dirty, my heart was in triathlon, so I didn't race on the mountain bike again that year. In fact it would be five years before I toed the line in an off- road race again in a twelve-hour team race with Aisling and incidentally finally got that first off-road win. But that's another story.

My first triathlon of the season was looming, so I put the mountain bike away and got ready. It was a sprint race, so it was not one that attracted all the very fast guys, but there was a handful. Being early in the year it was an indoor swim and I set a PB (personal best) Not a particularly fast one but a PB nonetheless. I went on to have a strong bike, moving up the field and for the first time ever held my place on the run. I finished in the top ten and was buzzing around like a ten-year-old who had just had too much sugar for about three days.

My next race was another sprint and it was my first outdoor swim with my newly-developed swimming skills. I couldn't wait. I was still on a high from my last result and I thought I could go top ten again that day. The weather was wet and windy and the sea was rolling and crashing. It looked a bit epic, even though it was only a 750-metre swim.

We made our way to the start and I went hard from the gun, but as soon as I turned at the buoy and swam parallel to the beach the waves were rolling me so badly that combined with me turning to breathe I started to get motion sickness. Sea sick in a triathlon – I just couldn't believe it! I reluctantly reverted to the breaststroke and made it through without getting any worse.

Then it was onto the bike, where I made up plenty of places lost during the swim and again I ran hard and even made up a few additional places. I finished in the top ten with the same buzz as last time, being just a little less like the ten-year-old with the sugar high.

The rest of the season followed a fairly similar pattern.

Depending on the size of the race I'd usually finish somewhere between fifth and thirtieth. I only once came close to a win, right at the end of the season in a small race but ended up third. It was my best result that far and sent me into the following winter motivated to train harder and race again the next year.

As it happened I stayed at a very similar level for the next season with only slight improvement. It seemed I'd found my limit, my place in the pecking order. There was one itch I needed to scratch though and I was planning on doing it the following year in Nice, France. I wanted a shot at trying to complete an Ironman.

CHAPTER 9
IRONMAN FRANCE JUNE 2008

My first attempt at doing an Ironman was in 2008 at Ironman France in Nice. I'd had the spark of desire since that day on the couch nearly fifteen years earlier. Finishing was my only target – cross the line, get the medal, tick that box and go back to short distance racing.

I'd read that doing an Ironman will change your life and we all want to do something that will magically transform us in some way, or maybe that's just me being naive. Perhaps I'm the only one who went into it thinking like that.

I was waiting for the moment of epiphany or enlightenment all through the race but as I crossed the finish line it just didn't arrive. There was no parting of clouds, no moment of enlightenment, no life-changing realisation. I was a little bit disappointed, euphoric yes, but still a little let down.

It wasn't until a couple of days later that the realisation dawned on me that it wasn't the race that changed me, it was the six months of training for the event. It was the complete change of lifestyle. The training, the discipline, learning about nutrition and the feeling of being really fit. I had also developed a deep sense of self-belief.

However, I'm getting ahead of myself. Let's take a step back to how I started that journey that ended up with my first Ironman medal hanging around my neck. Firstly I wanted that medal really badly, I wanted to cross the line and to complete the Ironman.

I entered and trained for the Dublin Marathon in 2007. I wanted to see if I could even manage just the running part of an Ironman on its own first. For an experienced runner a marathon isn't that big a deal, and it certainly it isn't that scary. For me as a beginner I was terrified standing there on the starting line. I had as much training done as I thought I needed, but I didn't know for sure and I was still afraid. I guess mostly it was the fear of failure but also of the pain and hitting the infamous wall and the difficulty and enormity of what I was about to attempt.

I think because I had such a fear and had wanted to complete a marathon for so long that by the time I got to the last 500 metres I was welling up and had a lump in my throat feeling just like the day I finished last in my first half Ironman. I just let the huge waves of emotion wash over me. I didn't try to suppress it and as long as I didn't start crying I was going to enjoy every second of this incredible feeling. I knew it would never feel the same again. No matter how many times you go on to cross the finishing line nothing comes close to your first time.

I walked very slowly down towards where the medals were being given out. I was moving slowly not only because I wanted the experience of elation to last, but also because every inch of my legs hurt more than I'd ever thought possible.

When I dipped my head so the girl could put the medal around my neck it was all I could do to swallow the rising lump in my throat and not let the emotion overwhelm me. At the same time I tried to lose myself in it. I met my family at the exit to the athletes' area and by that stage I was so sore and moving so slowly that I couldn't step up the kerb onto the footpath so I had to walk along in the gutter. I eventually just stopped, sat down and asked them to get the car and come back for me. I couldn't go any further. I sat there waiting with my medal resting on my chest full of the most glorious feelings of achievement, with a big stupid grin on my face. When they got back I needed help just to get back to my feet and into the car but that didn't matter.

I broke through another barrier not just physically but also in my mind. I didn't quite go home and enter the Ironman that day but in my head it was a done deal. I was going to do so. I was right back at the start of another journey as a complete beginner. I had no idea if I could complete an Ironman. It was even scarier than the marathon.

I started training properly in January for the race in June, the same time as I committed to it and entered. By that stage the bike shop had grown and it was much more specialist triathlon and much less of a regular bike shop. I had a sponsored team of eight athletes racing in our Wheelworx colours. A couple of them were very experienced long-course athletes so I had no shortage of advice and help.

My typical training week ran between six and ten hours but I was often inconsistent. Sometimes as a result of overdoing it and becoming too tired to keep on the training plan, I just trained however I felt on the day regardless of what the plan said. If I was down to do a two- hour easy ride and I went out and the sun was shining and I felt good I'd stay out for three or four hours often in the Dublin mountains which was my favourite place to ride. The result was a rest week that wasn't restful and the next week's training would suffer. It took me a long time to learn to do what I was told. I suppose that is a big part of why I work for myself. I don't like to be told what to do and I usually think I know best. In this instance it wasn't helping me a whole lot.

The other thing that got in the way of training was just life and in particular work. The race was on in June in the middle of one of the busiest times in the shop, so I was working long days and weeks and skipping sessions.

For my first Ironman most of the training time came from family time. I had the green card for this at the start, but I think neither of us had any idea of the effect it would have in reality either during the six months or afterwards. I learned lots during that period. I learned to love the discipline of getting the training done regardless of weather, mood or motivation. I loved the feeling of growing fitness and strength.

I used to do my big day of training on a Monday as it was my day off from work. I started in the morning with a two or three-kilometre swim with one of the athletes I sponsored. We then had breakfast before heading out for a 100km ride, followed by a ten-kilometre run straight afterwards.

I often didn't finish training until 5pm or later and at that stage I was in no shape to start cooking for the family who were due home shortly after that. This didn't always go down so well with my wife, who although supportive at the start ,understandably found it hard after months of disruption at home. To be found half comatose still in wet, sweaty and dirty kit on the couch when everyone arrived home shortly afterwards from work and school didn't go down well.

It became all-consuming . . . all I could think and talk about. That quickly became another source of tension at home so I kept most of my training and racing talk for work. Most athletes find that their first Ironman affects every part of their life, unlike anything else one could ever experience.

Every decision is made based around how it might affect the next training session or the recovery from the last. Like I said earlier I tend to go at things in a very 'full on' sort of way and often overdo it. This situation was no exception to that rule.

Even with my newfound love of training, discipline and my 'all in' attitude, I found that I eventually ran out of steam and four or five weeks before the race, motivation and desire headed out the back door and I found it impossible to get out training. I just wanted to race at this stage.

I'd had enough and wanted a break, but I wouldn't quite say I wanted my old life back.

CHAPTER 10
LIFE CHANGES AND IRONMAN
SWITZERLAND 2009

My life changed dramatically over the next year. My marriage of close to eighteen years ended and I entered a new relationship. Aisling my new partner was an elite international ultra runner and coincidentally had just completed her first Ironman. Being with someone who enjoyed training and racing as much as I did meant the lifestyle I'd come to love over the last year was easy to fit in.

I entered Ironman Switzerland the following year with the aim of becoming a lot faster, as I wanted to be competitive in my age group. I also thought that it would be a great idea to give Aisling an entry as a Christmas present. If you're looking for some advice, don't give an Ironman entry as a present to somebody unless that person specifically asks for it. She smiled politely and acted like it was a lovely and thoughtful present, exactly what she always wanted. It turned out however that it wasn't the best idea. Looking back at it now it seems obvious, but hindsight is a wonderful thing. I was in love with the sport and Ais had just done her first Ironman and loved the experience. I just assumed she would be as delighted with another entry as I was.

I began to train even harder than ever. My new life allowed me more time and I dreamed of being fast. I trained so much harder than the previous year that I expected big things from Switzerland and indeed I was faster. But that was really only down to it being a flatter, easier course and the temperature not being thirty-eight degrees on race day.

I finished 900th overall and 182nd in my age group. My swim was seven minutes slower, at 1:19:32. My bike at 5:40:35 was quicker by about forty minutes but that was mostly down to a faster bike course. My run too was faster but at 3:51:17 was not what I'd hoped for and again part of that could have been down to cooler conditions, although I'd managed to run the whole thing having learned from Aisling that walking during an Ironman marathon wasn't as inevitable as some would have you think. In fact walking in any marathon, including one at the back end of an Ironman was frowned upon – 'we're runners', I was told. 'We do not walk'.

I'd finished my second Ironman and had another nice shiny medal, but despite the elation and satisfaction, I was secretly disappointed if not completely surprised to discover that I hadn't become 'fast'.

CHAPTER 11
100K ULTRA

In 2010 Ais and I opened a new business. It was a 14,000 sq. ft. specialist triathlon and bike store in Dublin. As you would imagine it resulted in a huge workload for the first year and we took a break from Ironman.

We continued to run three or four times a week for forty to fifty minutes at a time, even at the craziest points of starting the new business. For the first five months we didn't take a day off and we worked an average of eighty hours a week, hitting 100 hours a couple of times. The running was more to keep us sane, a way to get a break from work and to try to just stay somewhat fit. It certainly wasn't what could have been called proper training.

One of the things that I love most about us as a couple is that we have never reached the point where we've had enough of each other and needed a break, despite the fact that we spend so much time together. The business was growing faster than we could have ever predicted and it was

CHASING KONA

a real roller coaster of a year trying to keep up with it.

At that time Aisling got a phone call from the selector of the Irish Ultra Running team who was going to race the Celtic Plate 100k. It's a Four Nations Championship race between Ireland, England, Scotland and Wales. Aisling had raced it before earning her first International place. This time she hadn't been training for anything long however, and the race was only five weeks away. We were driving home when we got the call and she covered the mouthpiece and asked me what I thought.

'Ask him if it's an open race as well as the championship, and if it is I'll do it with you', my mouth somehow managed to blurt out, before my brain had a chance to step in. She asked him and he confirmed it was open, so just like that we had five weeks to prepare for the longest ultra marathon I'd ever done.

Ais like I said had done the race before, and in fact she had gone much longer, having completed the 158k UTMB Ultra Trail du Mont Blanc in 2006. The UTMB is considered to be one of, if not the hardest footrace on the planet. It's a non-stop ultra marathon that starts in

Chamonix in the French Alps and races through both the Italian and Swiss Alps. At 9,600m vertical gain and loss it has more climbing and descending than Mount Everest.

In 2006 the time of the average finisher rate was just over 30 per cent. I think now it's still less than 50 per cent and it's significantly less than that for first-timers. Ais finished at her first attempt in 43 hours of non-stop climbing, running and descending in some of the most remote parts of the Alps. She still says it's the hardest thing she's ever done. I have believed almost since I met her that when it comes to racing and pushing herself up to and beyond her previous limits she is mentally the strongest person I've ever met. That leaves me in the conflicting position of having probably the best teacher possible beside me, but also someone a full foot shorter and almost twenty kilos lighter who was most likely going to kick my arse.

We thought we should get some training done. As we only had five weeks, the plan was that three would be building up and two of them would need to be tapering down. Our first attempt at a long run went against all conventional wisdom. We decided that as we (meaning Ais) were fairly experienced we would be ok to jump straight in with a three-hour run. I would just like to make this clear – this is not good advice! We lasted about two hours and forty minutes before we both decided that we'd had enough. Five weeks to train for a 100k race was looking like a stretch, a very big one.

I also blistered quite badly on that run for the first time that I can remember. When I pointed this out to Ais, not fully expecting but half hoping for sympathy, she smiled at me with an expression that said 'don't be a wuss' and told me it would be fine. I was far from convinced.

The plan was to run again the following morning after the previous day's attempt at a long session. Ais is a big believer in doing this as it teaches you to run on tired legs, which is an important skill to have when taking part in an ultra.

Not surprisingly the blisters hadn't miraculously healed by the next morning so I gingerly applied Vaseline and carefully put on my socks and runners before heading out. I hobble-ran for the first couple of minutes before realising that I couldn't feel the blisters at all. I shouldn't really have been surprised to discover that yet again Ais knew what she was talking about.

We continued to bring the mileage up quite quickly. The following week, running from home at the foot of the Dublin mountains to Enniskerry – a village about three- and-a-half hours and thirty-five kilometres away over the mountains – we set out with a bag, food, gels and water and some money for lunch and bus fare home. It was one of the most enjoyable runs I'd ever done. The next week we ran five hours to Roundwood, another small village in County Wicklow. Again we went over the mountains, mostly on trails, covering about fifty kilometres this time. Dad came down to meet us for lunch and bring us back home after that one.

These runs were really pleasant. Setting out with a bag on your back with food and drinks for the day feels like an adventure every time. It was great mentally, as we both felt that we could have managed six or seven hours the second time. So three long runs was about the extent of the specific preparation for the 100k. This was very far from ideal but there was no time left to do any more.

Race day came around and we had a plan in place regarding pacing. The plan was that Aisling was in charge. I had no problem with this because as I'd discovered while running my first ultra the previous year I hadn't got a clue when it came to pacing. I started way too fast and blew up fifty kilometres into a sixty-nine kilometre race. The last nineteen kilometres taught me a whole lot about how much somebody could suffer due to stupidity.

I still panicked a bit when we were dead last after the first kilometre, but I trusted Ais, so we stuck to the plan. We had Aisling's brother Eugene crewing for us and this was really important in such a long race. As you get further into the longer races it can be hard to keep track of what food or drink you've taken, so having someone telling you what to do and making decisions is a priceless asset, especially if you're as inexperienced as I was.

The race was on quiet country lanes and was made up of a lap of just over three kilometres. The short laps made nutrition fairly straightforward. We shared a bottle of carb or electrolyte drink at the start of most laps and carried a gel for halfway around. I had some minor stomach issues in the early laps that required a couple of toilet stops but that didn't really cause any big problems. Ais kept the pace really even with every lap clocking between eighteen and nineteen minutes.

Even the marathon distance came and went without incident, and Aisling's pacing strategy was working as we were picking off people and moving up the field. Fifty kilometres, then sixty kilometres, and the pace was still exactly the same. I was feeling really good and started to push a little at around sixty-five kilometres as we were caught by a friend of ours. He was also on the Irish team and he was a lot faster. I sped up a little to chat to him. I was feeling so good it couldn't do any harm. However, this was a stupid rookie mistake.

I started to struggle about five kilometres later. Coincidentally that was the time that Ais was starting to feel ready to race. So as I slowed, she got progressively faster.

I dug in and tried to get more food and drink in on the next two laps but that didn't work and I felt sick as well as sore and slowed a bit more. I only took on water for the next few laps and the stomach started to feel better. I couldn't go any faster but at least I was still running.

I calculated somewhere around the eighty-five kilometre mark that Ais was likely to catch and lap me. I was losing two or three minutes a lap on the pace we had been doing and she was going about one minute quicker.

Sure enough with two laps to go Ais caught and passed me and she was flying. I was really struggling but I did – as I had expected – get a good lift from seeing her running well and her big happy smile and her shout of 'Hey Lovely Bob'. This is what she calls me. And before you ask it's because I am lovely. Well she thinks so anyway! Some guys get cool nicknames like The Rock or The Hammer. I'm simply Lovely Bob.

Like I said, I was struggling really badly but had made it to ninety-eight kilometres with no walking. I hadn't been able to take on food for a long time because I felt sick, so I was completely empty. I couldn't even begin to describe how sore my legs were. And it was not just my legs. One of the things they don't tell you about running ultras, particularly as a beginner, is that everything hurts. My arms hurt from holding them in the normal position they'd be in while I ran but they had been doing that for nearly ten hours. My head, feet, hands, I think even my ears hurt. Don't ask me how, they just did.

Every step sent fresh jolts of pain and hurt through every part of my body. Time and distance had somehow slowed down, so that seconds seemed to take minutes. I started to retch but there was nothing in my stomach. I was still sort of running, but my eyes kept closing and when I opened them I'd find myself on the far side of the road still shuffle-running and not sure how far I'd gone, while almost blacking out and still moving.

I retched again and had to stop while trying not to throw up. I got going and opened my eyes to realise I was 20 metres further down the road. After what seemed like ages but was probably only five or six minutes of walking a bit, retching, jogging, cramping, retching and walking again I slowly started to recover.

I tried to start running very easy and this time the cramping and nausea held off. For the last kilometre I actually managed to pick up the pace to something resembling a proper run.

Crossing the line was a huge sense of relief. For so long all I had wanted to do was to stop moving, just stop, and lie down.

Ais was finished just over forty-five minutes before me and in the process had made her way up to fourth place. She was catching up to both third and second, but ran out of road and time. It's a bit hard to believe, but I think 100k is almost too short for her and I think she will do even better at longer distances.

I was delighted to finish and even more chuffed at being able make it to ninety-eight kilometres before having to walk. I loved this race. We both had a great day out and I would very much like to go back and try hanging on to Ais a bit longer to get closer to her time . . . maybe even hang on with her to the finish.

In the end I finished in ten hours and thirteen minutes and Ais was nine hours and twenty-seven minutes. There have been several 'Ah-Ha' moments since, where I have gained a new belief or have had a new insight or have pushed back the mental barriers and boundaries of what I previously thought was possible.

Before this race a marathon seemed like a really long way. After running 100k it now looks short. Probably most importantly it looks short at the back end of an Ironman. I was to take this new perspective into my next Ironman race and it made for a very different experience to any that I'd participated in before. I have found again and again that my perspective on things changes after I do something so demanding or achieve something so thrilling. Much less often am I in awe of others watching them do what had seemed impossible to me in the past.

CHAPTER 12
A COACH AND BELIEF

I shouldn't have any reason to think I can qualify for the Ironman World Championships in Kona. It's reserved for the top two to three per cent of the world's fastest fittest Ironman triathletes in the world. With the exception of a couple of very small local events I don't win races. I don't even win my age group and in the bigger races I come nowhere.

In March of 2010 I didn't let any of that get in the way of asking Ais if she thought that qualifying for Kona was a realistic target for me and she in turn didn't let any of it get in the way of telling me she thought I could. If she had said 'Rob you're dreaming, cop yourself on', I would have moved on and it would have remained nothing more than a daydream to entertain me during my training rides and runs.

Ais believed I could get to Kona long before I did, and more importantly she believed it long before I had done anything that would normally lead someone to that conclusion. So in the absence of actually believing in myself I just trusted in her belief in me. In March we both entered Ironman UK, which was on in July. That gave us about five months training before the race. I had been off the bike and out of the pool for about a year, while concentrating on the new business. We were running fit but that's a very different thing to being ready to complete, never mind race an Ironman. It would be a fairly big request for someone who was already a fast triathlete aiming to get back into shape. For me, as a back of the pack triathlete to get to a level where I would be in the top seven or eight of my age group and inside the top fifty overall in a race with over 2000 participants was almost a ridiculous target.

The biggest part of making the decision to try to qualify was Aisling's belief that I could do it. Looking at the numbers it was a completely irrational idea, if not a fantasy. In my first Ironman I finished in the bottom quarter of the field, taking almost twelve-and-a-half hours, coming 240th in my age group and 951st overall.

That put me almost three hours and over 900 places away from qualifying, according to last year's IMUK results.

My second attempt in Ironman Switzerland – after a big increase in training – moved me up a grand total of 51 places overall. Qualifying would therefore only require an improvement of about 860 places, not to mention having to go an hour faster on a much harder, slower course. Ironman UK is renowned as being one of the hardest and hilliest Ironman races in Europe and it's a much slower course than my last race in Zurich where I had barely broken eleven hours. This one needed to have a nine at the start of the finishing time and I was also going to have to make that improvement in only five months.

I tried telling myself that I wasn't that far off the qualifying standard if you looked at the individual sports. The reality though was that I was a long way short when you had to put them together on race day – a very long way off.

Swim: Just over an hour.

Bike: About 5.5 hours at an average speed of 32-33kph. Run: I would then need a 3:20 marathon.

Add in two transitions and it all added up to just under ten hours. Like I said, I wasn't that far off doing them individually as fast as I would need to qualify, but doing any of them at the required speed would have me at my limit. I kept telling myself that putting them together should be achievable and I just needed to find the 'magic bullet' that would push me onto the next level.

By way of background, let me tell you a little bit about Aisling. Actually by the end of this book I'll have told you quite a bit about her as she has again and again been a hugely pivotal and influential part of my story. Anyway, there are, to my mind, two types of people. There's the type who when you entrust them with something such as an idea or a dream you might have they may scoff, or maybe while seeming to agree that it's a good idea they go on to point out all of the reasons why someone like you couldn't or shouldn't do something. The other type of person is the one who listens to your idea and tells you to go for it. They encourage you and make you believe that even if it's going to be a stretch for you that you should try anyway. They start to suggest ideas, places to start or ways to do it. That second type of person describes my Aisling. The other important thing to point out about Ais is that if she thinks it's a bad idea or a pipe dream she will usually tell me, quite quickly.

So Ais believed in me and I trusted her. That was enough to start with, but we didn't really have a next step. The problem was neither of us knew what that next action should be. Obviously I needed to swim, bike and run but there was more to it that that. How much should I swim and how far and what type of sessions? Open water or pool? Coached or club or group or solo? All of the same questions and more applied to the bike and funnily enough to the run. Then there was the question of how to mix the sessions. How many hard ones? Should I train hard twice one day then easy the next day? Or maybe train hard for two or three days, followed by a couple of easy ones? How many hours a week would I need to train? Ten, fifteen, twenty or thirty? We had no idea. There were many more questions than answers.

So I took the obvious next step and I had a word with Google and came back with 27,000,000 answers, most of which contradicted each other. 'I qualified on an average of six hours training a week,' claimed one search result. 'The average Kona qualifier trains eighteen to twenty hours a week, but thirty-plus hour weeks aren't unheard of,' said another.

My favourite was this one, from one of the most useful resources I've found on Ironman training. It's a website called www.endurancecorner. com and the article is written by one of their contributors and coaches, a triathlete himself, called Alan Couzens.

According to VO2max data from the Cooper institute, Kona qualifiers are in the top 0.5%-.0025% of the population when it comes to fitness. In other words, if you're a young (college age guy) and we randomly sampled 200 folks from your dorm, you would consistently be the fittest. Taking this a little further, if you're a 40-something guy living in a pretty good-sized town of 40,000 people, you're the fittest guy in town! This kind of stat doesn't happen without living a little differently to those 39,999 folks who have more 'normal' fitness.

Jesus, that's a tall order, not to mention a fairly wide range of answers to the original question! I had narrowed the required training down to somewhere between six and thirty hours a week. And then I only needed to become the fittest person I know.

Ais being the clever half of the equation decided the thing to do was to find someone who knew the answers and could teach us what we needed to know, or better yet, to coach me. We knew of someone that fitted the bill. He was a very experienced triathlete who had raced as a high level professional and was now coaching. I had known him for a couple of years and he's what I think of as a very 'instinctual' type of coach. He hadn't just learned it all in a classroom or from a textbook. I'd seen him make observations on athletes' form and technique after watching them run for a couple of hundred metres. He had a very good trained eye and a really good understanding of training and technique. More importantly, he knew if it was something that should be fixed or left alone. If it was something that needed to be changed he knew what drills or exercises were needed to do that too. We'd seen him have very good success with a number of athletes and we both thought he was the one to ask. So we asked him and he promptly said it wasn't possible!

Maybe if I did two years of serious training, but probably even then he didn't think five months was realistic. That only slowed us for a second before changing approach and asking if he knew how to coach someone who had the ability to get to Kona. He said 'yes', of course he knew how to do that. We asked him to disregard what he thought about my ability or chances and coach me as he would someone whom he believed could do it. He thought about it briefly before agreeing. I think he thought we were both either stupid or crazy, but he decided that he'd take me on.

I'd learned something about belief from Aisling. If you just start to take the same steps that someone who can already do what you want to achieve, you can get there despite not really believing at the start. Belief often follows action. It doesn't matter whether you believe in the possibility at the beginning or not. You just need to start.

I'd learned this lesson from Ais the previous year when I was less than a month away from my first ultramarathon. I was really struggling with doubts whether I could do it or not. It was a sixty-nine-kilometre race in France (Ais of course being a much more experienced ultrarunner kept calling it only a 'short ultra', which wasn't helping with my self esteem) I was worried. Driving home from another race one evening I sort of let slip that I was more than a little concerned.

What if I don't finish? What if I can't finish? What if...? I blubbered uncontrollably. Now that I'd started I didn't seem to be able to control my stupid mouth. Ais cut across me in mid- sentence. 'What if you had to get out of the car right now and make your own way home? What then? Would you just sit at the side of the road and stop and feel sorry for yourself?'

It wasn't a threat, just her pragmatic way of teaching me something. At least I don't think it was a threat because we were about forty-five kilometres from home at that point and it would have been a long way to go in the dark. 'Well, no,' I said. 'I'd start running.'

'And if you couldn't run anymore?', she asked. 'What then? Would you stop and give up?'

'No, at that stage I guess I'd walk till I could run again.' 'But you'd make it home?'

'Yeah, of course,' I answered and then the penny dropped.

'Well that's what you do in the race. You just keep moving until you get to the end.'

It was really only after that short conversation that I started to believe I could do it. But I'd taken the decision to enter and do the race months ago, long before I believed I could do it. I'd started taking steps towards the goal. We now had most of the ingredients needed to give me the best chance to succeed. All that was left was to start taking the steps. Time was ticking. It was now just over four months to go.

CHAPTER 13
SIMPLE, NOT EASY

The coach got stuck in straight away and didn't hold back. He was either going to beat me into submission and break me in the process or get me into good enough shape to qualify. He was running a training camp the

following weekend and suggested that if myself and Ais could get the time off from the shop we should come along. We did and it started the biggest nine days of training I'd ever done, clocking up almost thirty-three hours, including a sprint triathlon. The sprint race was on day eight of that first nine-day block. I should have been exhausted, especially as I cycled over an hour to get to it, but instead I finished third overall and won my age group. It was my best finish ever and my first age group win. With almost thirty hours training in my legs, I was sure I'd come nowhere and only be doing the race as a training exercise.

To show how different that nine-day training block was from anything I'd done before and to put it into context, my previous three-and-a-half weeks training hours looked like this:

Before the coach

March 2011

Week 1

Total hours 4:50

Swim 2:35 6400m 4 sessions

Bike 1:30 32k 1 session

Run 45 minutes 8.5k 1 session

Week 2

Total hours 9:40

Swim 2:35 7800m 3 sessions

Bike 4:55 160k 2 sessions

Run 2:10 23.5k 2 sessions

Week 3

Total hours 11:45

Swim :30 1100m 1 session

Bike 10:00 268k 4 sessions

Run 1:15 15.5k 3 sessions

Week 4

Total hours 16:30

Swim 1:00 2300m 1 session

Bike 11:20 281k 4 sessions

Run 4:10 49.5k 4 sessions

I started working with the coach in week 5. The first session he gave me was on Saturday, which was when we were on his training camp. As a result most of this weeks' hours were in the last two days of the week. Of the 19h25mins training done that week Saturday and Sunday totalled 12h30.

After the coach started
Week 5
Total hours 19:25
Swim 4:50 9700m 6 sessions
Bike 8:40 230k 3 sessions
Run 5:55 62k 5 sessions

Week 6
Total hours 20:30
Swim 4:00 11100m 5 sessions
Bike 11:10 323k 6 sessions
Run 5:20 61k 5 sessions

Up to the end of week 6 totalled the biggest training load I'd ever done by a long way. Nine days, 33 hours and I had my best race result on day eight of this block. I was stunned. I thought I had discovered the 'magic bullet' we are all searching for and it was so simple – just train lots. But simple does not mean easy. In fact I was to learn that sometimes simple is very, very hard.

At around the same time we were approached by a newspaper wanting to write a feature about Aisling the success of the new business and how she still managed to fit in her training and run at an elite level. When Ais asked about whether I would be needed for the interview the answer made it clear in a polite sort of way that an ordinary back of the pack triathlete who ran a triathlon shop was not newsworthy so I wasn't required.

I said nothing and just smiled. Inside I stewed and thought of the journalist, 'I'll show you'. At the same time we had been working with one of the biggest Irish outdoors sports magazines. I helped with content for product testing and reviews and we had become good friends with the editor. I suggested to Ais a while after her newspaper interview that maybe there might be interest in a series of articles in the Outsider magazine following my progress trying to qualify for Kona. She thought it was a good idea, so we approached Vanessa the editor who was very supportive and despite the seemingly impossible task I'd set myself, she decided to run with it. So now not only was I taking on a major challenge that no one except Aisling believed I could do, but I was going to announce my intention in a national publication. I figured that in the worst-case scenario we would get some good publicity for the shop. It's amazing how motivating that series of articles became over the next couple of months when I didn't feel like training. There were a lot of days that the fear of public humiliation was more than enough to get my runners or bike shoes on and to get moving.

April was really my first full month of proper training working with the new coach, and I totalled over ninety hours. This was probably a 300 per cent increase over any month I'd done before. I averaged over twenty hours most weeks with the longest being over twenty-five hours. It remained one of my most intense months from a training point of view. The other numbers for the month were:

April 2011

Total Training hours 91:10

Swim 18:25 35600m 14 sessions

Bike 52:00 1359km 19 sessions

Run 20:45 226km 16 sessions

May started out in a similar vein with another twenty-hour week, before dropping drastically to seven hours in week

2. This wasn't completely as planned. It was just that I was exhausted from the lprevious six weeks and couldn't keep hitting the sessions. The coach didn't seem to be surprised by this. In fact he was probably more

surprised that I had lasted as long as I had before going into meltdown. He adjusted the programme, taking all of the hard and long sessions out for the week and dropping most bike and runs, but left in all the swims, actually adding in a couple of extras. With the exception of one three-kilometre swim they were all very short. By keeping in the frequency it helped me continue to work on my weakest area, my swimming technique, without the physical load of hard sessions.

The easy week had the desired effect and I started to recover, but instead of getting back to the training plan after that, work and life interfered. I missed sessions and the ones I did were cut short. I ended up with only three hours training from Monday to Saturday. The following day, Sunday we were starting an eight-day bike sportive event which was to be a key block in my training.

Consistency is one of the most important aspects of Ironman training and for a long time it was an area with which I struggled. Either because I overdid it in training and wasn't fully recovered for the next session or I got busy at work and instead of reducing my training volume I stopped altogether. Getting to Kona doesn't require superhuman talent. It only requires that you train a lot of hours consistently for a very long period of time. It's a very simple concept that's very hard to implement. We not only had to push up to but often to exceed my limits in trying to stretch my ability far enough. At the same time we had to make sure we didn't go so far that I couldn't continue training.

It's all about the big picture. It matters much less what specific session you do on any given day in the pool, whether it is hard or easy, fast or slow. What mattered more was that I was there every Monday and Wednesday and Thursday and Friday. What also mattered was being able to fit in an average of three or four hours of training a day, six days a week, every week for probably ten months in a year. It all came down to how much I wanted it. My Dad calls it 'having a fire in your belly'. Ais says it's about desire, of wanting and needing something so badly that you will do whatever it takes to achieve it. How badly do you want it, how hard are you willing to work to get there and how many 'sacrifices' are you willing to make along the way?

I don't for one minute believe that you need natural talent. According to my laboratory tests I certainly don't have enough. What I had was a burning desire to get there. I'd wanted it for probably fifteen years at the time.

If you want something badly enough you make it happen. I realised that the secret wasn't in the training plan. The secret to Ironman is how can you fit the training into your daily life.

One of the things I love about Ironman is the discipline. Not just the discipline of the training, but also learning to apply that discipline to the other parts of my life. Organising everything in advance has been one of the big keys to being able to sustain the level of training and work that both myself and Aisling do. We sit down at the start of the week and plan how we are going to fit everything in. The things that have to be done get slotted in first, like work. Then we start looking at where we can fit in training. Then we put in time off. The benefit of doing it like this is that there are no surprises for either of us. There are clear boundaries set for training, work and home life. We are lucky that we are both involved in the sport, so there isn't any explanation as to why I need to get in another six-hour bike ride or why Ais needs to do a three-hour run. But if you are taking on the challenge of a first Ironman or deciding that you are going to chase Kona, it's very easy to get your partner excited about the enormity of the challenge of the day for you. What's more important is that they are aware of the fact that 95 per cent of an Ironman is done every day for the six to twelve months before you set foot on the starting line and that it will most likely have a huge effect on their life as well as yours. I think it's best to be completely clear from the start about what's going to be required.

Like I said, I'm lucky that we are both heavily involved in sport, but I still organise my weeks training ahead of time with Ais, so there are no surprises. It's one of the simplest things we do but is one of the most important lessons I've learnt and one of the keys to being able to make sport a long-term sustainable lifestyle for both of us.

CHAPTER 14
TRAINING CAMPS, PUSHING LIMITS

In May myself and Ais were entered in an eight-day 1200km bike challenge. It wasn't a race but a sportive, and it was to be a key part of my training. It consisted of a huge overload of biking, but at a steady level. As a result the bulk of my swimming and running were cut, with only one session of each done in the eight days.

I experienced a great physical response to the week on the bike, feeling stronger as the days went on, but I was very tired afterwards and again I struggled to keep going. The two weeks after the massive bike week my training fell off the face of the earth again. Monday, Tuesday and

Wednesday we did nothing at all. Thursday we met the coach for our weekly session in the Phoenix Park and did an hour's run with some hard intervals. Friday we did an hour's easy running, but I felt really tired. Saturday we ran again for an hour with some hard efforts. The following week we were getting ready for a two-week training camp in France and as usual work was manic between catching up from the week off in May and getting ready for the training camp the following week.

Myself and Ais had hired an apartment just outside Nice in the south of France and were going to put in a big block of volume of all three sports. I think looking back at the training hours I managed on the camp I was nowhere near recovered enough to do another two weeks of big volume training, but this was unknown territory for all of us and while we knew it was risky we didn't feel we had too much choice. Because of the very restrictive timeline we had set we were always going to be pushing the limits of what I could handle and often crossed that line.

The first week was the hardest mentally. Often just getting out the door was an absolute killer but the coach had told me to stay in daily contact by text and he was brilliant at reading my mood and motivating me to keep going, even when all I wanted was to sleep by the pool. One day I had a ninety-minute tempo run after a three- hour bike ride on the schedule and I had been putting the run off. I hadn't felt too bad on the bike just tired and sick of the constant workload. The coach texted to check on how I was doing and after ascertaining that I wasn't physically over the edge, he told me to put on my runners and go for a fifteen-minute run. 'Just see how you feel. If you're that bad just cut the session and take the rest of the day off,' he said. I very reluctantly did as I was told and was amazed to find that about ten minutes in I started to feel good. I went on to do the session exactly as was scheduled.

It was a good lesson to learn. Just because I didn't feel like going out didn't mean I shouldn't, and if I was actually too tired to train I could just cut the session off and turn back after ten or fifteen minutes. A twenty-minute slow easy run is unlikely to tip you over the edge of overtraining, but it will confirm if you are just mentally tired, in which case an easy run will often do good. I was learning to read the body's signals, telling me whether or not I was going too far. I think I was regularly overreaching, stretching past my body's limits but only to a point from which I could recover. Up to then I hadn't reached a point of overtraining.

The body has warning signals when you're overdoing it and for me my sleep was one of the first things to be affected if I was pushing too far. Mood is another one of my early warning systems. I get very cranky when

I'm reaching the tipping point of doing too much. There are lots of other signals, but I have learned to monitor both of these closely and I now track them in my training log. I can then see patterns emerging as sleep gets poor or mood and motivation is low, so I know I'm reaching a limit. I was learning that I could live with a level of overreaching for a certain length of time without going over the edge. I would usually recover from it in a matter of days. All I needed was a reduction in volume or intensity or a day or two off. Overtraining is very different and can take weeks or months to get over. I hit just under fifty-five hours training in the two weeks and although it was less than I'd hoped to do it was all adding up. I was way too tired at that stage to feel all the positive effects. I just had to trust in the coach and trust that what I had been doing was going to come good in time for the big event in July.

CHAPTER 15
THE LAST PUSH – HELL OF THE WEST TRIATHLON – KILKEE, 2011

My first real test race to see if I had any chance of qualifying for Ironman UK (IMUK), which was now only four weeks away, was going to be the Hell of the West triathlon in Kilkee. It is one of the most testing Olympic distance races in Ireland and always attracts a very competitive field. I was nervously excited. I was in much better shape than ever before and I was hoping at least to get into the top twenty. I knew that there would be a lot of guys there targeting this as their number one 'A' race. I was sort of training through it, but with very little taper or reduction in training load. As a result I would have been very happy to have been up close to the front of the field but had no illusions of anything more ambitious, at a distance that I wasn't expressly targeting.

The day didn't quite go as planned. In fact it's probably more accurate to say it was a complete disaster. I was 293rd out of the water. I've never been a strong swimmer, but this was worse than I used to be. I spent the rest of the race moving steadily up the field but only finished 93rd.

I was very disappointed and reality hit me really hard. How could I race Ironman UK in a matter of weeks and expect to be at the top of the field in a triathlon almost four times as long and much more competitive? How could I have trained so hard and had such a bad result?

I had to put it down as a bad day. I just had to keep on training and hope for the best. Despite the result a tiny part of me still believed I was in much better shape than the day showed. Aisling agreed and all the way home we dissected the race and the preparation, trying to come up with an answer. In the end we decided the best thing was to write it off and to keep following the plan.

I think the coach recognised that I was reaching the limit of what I could not only do in training but what I could actually absorb. But he also knew that I wasn't ready to qualify for IMUK in less than four weeks. There was going to be one more push, despite how exhausted I was. The next five days had only very short recovery sessions, and training consisted mainly of short bikes and swims. The respite was short-lived and Saturday saw me do my longest bike ride of just over 200k and a thirty-minute hard run off that. Sunday was a two-hour swim followed by a two-hour run before work. The next nine days totalled thirty-one hours. I alternated between complete exhaustion one day and feeling superhuman the next. I'd have a four-kilometre swim when I felt strong and fast and could go all day. The next day it was all I could do to manage to force myself to stay in the pool and drag myself through a three-kilometre easy swim.

I struggled through one more big week of just under twenty hours and it was all done. I would never have believed before that I could push myself so hard for so long. I never would have believed that I could continue to train with the level of exhaustion I'd had for over two months now. I had run out of time and all that was left was a two-week taper and to toe the starting line in a fortnight. I discovered I had a problem at this stage because I had programmed my head during dozens of exhausted hard training hours that I only needed to reach this point and that then I was done. However, I still had two weeks of lighter training to go, albeit at a much lower volume, but I couldn't stop. Mentally I found this one of the hardest times. I had no motivation to do any training and the business that had been neglected for the last number of months was in the middle of our busiest period. I had a lot of catching up to do and fought every easy excuse not do do the last few sessions. Ais was great, as always. She kicked my arse or cajoled me into keeping on training, knowing which would work at any given time, which was usually the arse-kicking.

I had six of the easiest days training I'd had in four months and then I had a couple of key sessions during the weekend before the race, a 4000m time trial being the first. I always have this horrible nervous fear going into what I know is going to be a hard testing session and I was dreading this one all week. I had no idea where my swimming was, as I was always so tired in training. It went incredibly well and I knocked lumps off not only my four- kilometre PB but also off my 1500m and 400m PBs along the way. I got out of the water on such a high I texted the TT numbers to the coach from the changing room. I couldn't wait to call him later. The next day was a one- hour pace run to be run just faster than my target Ironman pace. Again I expected it to hurt and had that nervous fear in my belly driving to the track. When I started it was so easy to hit the time targets that I found myself again on a huge high. I cruised through the workout faster than I'd hoped, feeling like I was flying.

So there was only one week to go. The last week was only swimming and biking and despite – or probably as a result of – the fantastic workouts I'd had over the weekend I had zero motivation to train. I did a couple of very short swims and bikes before loading up the car and heading for the ferry.

CHAPTER 16
AUGUST 2011 IRONMAN U.K
BOLTON 2011

Afficterm the disastrous result in my last triathlon in Kilkee and the fact that some of my training had been a bit hit and miss I and the coach still weren't sure that I was ready for the challenge ahead. I wasn't quite at qualification standard. As a result, we started thinking that it was going to be a 'B' race, meaning that I would aim to get straight back into training and have IM Florida in

November – three months away – as my backup and probably more realistically as my main 'A' race, and with my best chance of qualifying. Instead of the rushed four- month run-in, I would have about seven months in total and the experience of another Ironman under my belt.

This was a good indication of how nervous we were all feeling at this stage. The taper had gone well though and despite the thought that I wasn't ready by the time race day came around, my confidence was high. I'd had a couple of really successful test sessions in the last week, felt rested and fresh for the first time in months and was the most relaxed I'd ever been at a race.

As the race day got closer Ais and I did everything possible to have the last week's preparation as close to perfect as possible. From the taper and carb loading to a short work week we tried to make sure everything within our power was perfect. On Friday we drove the bike course and I started to think that it was made for me. It's really technical, with lots of junctions, corners, rolling hills and a couple of decent climbs. I was also looking forward to the hilly run.

I spent a couple of hours polishing and cleaning my bike, fitting new bar tape, new tyres and taking it for a test ride. It's part of my pre-race ritual now and one I really enjoy. The lads in the shop have it serviced and ready to ride, but I always go through the last checks myself. I find it very relaxing and it's another box ticked in the preparation. I always think you're as well to go through everything about race day in your head beforehand. I spend time alone visualising each thing I need to do. I write it down and cross each item off the list as I do it. That way I don't forget anything and leave as little as possible to chance. I think it's a big part of making your own luck, by eliminating as much of the 'bad' luck as possible through good preparation. You also need to be flexible as things might not always go your way, but the more prepared I am the better I am able to cope when things go wrong.

Ais and I perform a ritual of writing a message on each other with a permanent marker before we leave for the race start in the morning. Whenever I see it during the day it gives me a lift, knowing I have a little piece of her racing with me on the day. It's often nothing more than a black smudge by the time I get to the run but it still gives me huge confidence.

IMUK race day

I like to get to transition and the start early on race day. That way I stay relaxed and usually avoid the extra stress of rushing around trying to get everything done at the last minute. We got to the race site while it was still dark, so race day itself started with a strange level of calm. Everyone has their pre-race routines and I'm no different. I like to walk through transition in the exact way I will be racing in a couple of hours and I do this alone, usually wearing a running cap pulled down low to hide my face and headphones on, with a pre-race playlist kicking in my head. I don't want to meet anyone I know at this stage and start talking as it's a hugely important part of my race preparation that I always do uninterrupted and I do it all in my head. I see it like a movie, rehearsing where my bag is in the transition tent. I take it down and empty it, then put on my helmet, glasses and shoes. I then take them back off, replace the bag ready for the race and do it over in my head slowly and deliberately with my eyes closed another three or four times. I will often walk the route into the tent two or three times up to my bag so I don't miss it in the excitement of the race.

Then I walk out to where my bike is racked, noting any landmarks at the end of my rack or counting them if there isn't one. I walk over and take my bike and walk the route I'm going to take to the exit. Then after I re-rack it I do it over again, eyes closed in my head until I feel calm and ready.

I had decided to race without a watch as I felt it was better not to know if I'd had a bad swim time as it might affect me mentally and how hard I would push for the rest of the day. It was the first time I had done this. The weather was perfect. It was warm and overcast and forecasted to stay that way all day. I kissed Ais, wished her good luck and swam out for the deep water start.

Despite previous poor swim starts I nervously took the advice of my coach, and went right to the front. I had savage butterflies in my stomach as we treaded water for a couple of minutes before the countdown and then the gun sounded and we were off.

I started fast to try and get away from the scrum at the start and quickly settled into a hard pace but one that I hoped I could sustain. The water was quite warm and the swim went well. I spent long periods drafting in small packs and felt I swam hard the whole way. I got out of the water knowing I had done all I could in terms of effort. I just had to hope it was good enough. I didn't see the clock as I exited so didn't find out till after the race that I had a swum a PB of 1h02. I ran into T1 and despite all of my mental preparation, I grabbed Aisling's bag instead of mine. I had to run back to change it. Then in my panic to make up for the lost time I made a bit of a mess of putting on my shoes and fumbled like a beginner with my helmet. I swore I'd do better next time. I ran through transition as I had planned with no more mishaps and started very steadily on the bike. I occupied my mind with correct pacing, thinking about my nutrition and riding as smart as possible.

The hardest part of the first thirty minutes was getting passed by quite a few people. I argued with myself that I knew how I should feel at this stage. I knew I was riding the correct pace for me and that they were either faster than me, in which case I shouldn't race them, or they were starting too fast and in that case I'd see them again soon enough. Indeed I saw them all again, mostly in the first hour. I think the most valuable lesson I've learned about racing or even just completing an Ironman is just how easy it feels at the start of the bike and how much self restraint it takes not to race as hard as you 'feel' you can or should for the first thirty or forty kilometres. I was constantly moving up through the field but had no idea how far up.

On the third lap part of the course I loved the climb and the descent and I knew both were an area to make up time, so I pushed a bit harder. My bike racing experience came in handy on this course, as I was able to save lots of time by cornering well. Even saving seconds through each of the dozens of corners would make a difference at the end of the day. When we looked at both my and Aisling's bike computers I had ridden two kilometres less than she had, all down to taking better lines through corners and on the descents.

On the third lap I was still catching people but much less than before. I had passed some of the pro women and with less than ten kilometres to go I caught Desiree Flicker, who had gone into the race as one of the favourites. When I recognised who she was I got such a huge rush of adrenaline and emotion to realise that I was actually passing her. I was near the front of the field, but what I didn't know at the time was that she wasn't leading and was actually having a bad day. But like I said, I didn't know that at the time. All I knew then was that it had given me a huge lift at the end of the bike course when I was sore and tired. I finished the bike and entered transition two and it was almost empty. It was at that moment that I really started to believe I could do it. For the first time I wasn't just saying the words, trying to force myself to believe in what I was doing. Yes, I was indeed doing it.

I flew through transition and out onto the run. My legs felt great from the beginning, but both Ais and the coach warned me not to go hard at the start. 'Do the first ten kilometres easy, then pick it up and race for as long as you can,' is what they said. I had grabbed my Garmin in transition as I was still very inexperienced at run pacing and didn't trust myself to do this part on feel. I had it set to lap every kilometre and it just kept on beeping. Another kilometre done, and another and another. I loved the feeling of moving so well and I was still catching and passing people and that was giving me a big lift all over again. The main lap of the run course is about ten kilometres out from T2 then you do three laps through the town of . I felt like an over-excited pup straining on its lead. I was counting down the kilometres until the ten- kilometre mark, where I'd been told I could pick it up. I didn't last that long. At eight kilometres I picked up the pace a little and I just couldn't help myself I felt so good. I held it at that pace for a couple of minutes and still felt good and still the Garmin kept on beeping telling me that another one had been done. Then I got onto the lap section and gave it another nudge and held that pace for another few minutes to see how it felt. I felt invincible.

The K's just flew by and I kept on passing people. I was smiling and nodding 'hello' at all of the aid station volunteers and the spectators and getting a big boost from them smiling back. This is one of the most valuable lessons I've ever learned. I'm convinced it's why thirteen- times Ironman winner and four-times Ironman World Champion Chrissie Wellington smiles throughout all of her races.

The crowd love it and smile back and cheer and the lift you get from it is better than any energy drink or gel. I kept on making eye contact and smiling at people on the first lap and they remembered it the next time and cheered for me. Then I saw Ais coming onto the run course and that gave me an even bigger lift, as she was grinning ear-to-ear loving being on her feet and she was flying. The middle twenty-three kilometres flew by effortlessly. There was no pain and no hurt and I was on such a high from the crowd and the fact that I was actually racing an Ironman, not simply just completing it. I even caught some of the male professionals. I just kept on running on the high of the adrenaline and endorphin buzz.

At about thirty-two kilometres it all of a sudden went from feeling like Superman to feeling like someone had driven over my legs with a truck. The pain went from being mild background noise to all consuming in a matter of seconds. I took a gel and coke and dug in hard, harder than I've ever gone. I saw the clock as I passed the finishing line heading out on my last lap and I knew I was not only on target to beat 10:07 which was last year's last qualifying slot, but if I hung on I was going to have a finish time starting with a nine. On the last lap when I really hurting, the smiles and cheers from the crowd that I had put in the bank was worth its weight in gold. It gave me such a boost and kept me digging in. Despite the pain going deeper and deeper into the hurt I used the smiles and cheers to drive me harder. I didn't want to disappoint them after they'd supported me all day. Then I'd see Ais and she'd shout at me that I was flying and dig in and of course there was the huge smile every time. She's always smiling when she's running. She was also moving faster than almost everyone else on the course and at that stage and looked so impressive.

With only three kilometres to go I started to feel very sick, along with experiencing increasing pain, but I just kept telling myself to push for just one more minute and that then I could slow down. I'd get that minute and ask myself for another one and then I was into the last kilometre and I was running as hard as I could, being swept along by the huge support and my rising emotions. I ran into the finishing chute and crossed the line in 9h49.

I still had no idea if that was enough. I had no idea of my place, so after asking the race director and being told that the results were going up online live I went to get my phone. Opening the athlete tracker it said I had finished fifth in my age group and thirty-sixth overall. I couldn't believe it. That meant with seven provisional slots, I'd qualified for the world championships.

I headed back onto the course to watch Ais and when she ran past I shouted my placing at her and told her that I'd qualified. She looked as delighted as I was. A short while later I made my way back into the finishing area to meet her coming across the line. It was a massive PB for her and she finished in 11:40, over one hour and forty-five minutes faster than her previous best time. Along the way she also clocked the third fastest women's marathon time of 3h07, being only beaten by two of the professional women. She also set personal best's in both other disciplines as well as being the fastest Irish woman.

I had spoken to my coach on the phone and he told me the athlete tracker information was wrong. I was still thirty-sixth overall, but I was actually eighth in my category, not fifth, as I believed. That meant I was relying on one slot to roll down, as there had been seven places listed for my age group.

We rode the emotional roller coaster of being in and then out, then not knowing for the rest of the day and all night. I didn't sleep much and was at the awards ceremony early the following morning, hoping that my luck would hold. When we arrived we got two surprises. Ais was actually fourth in her category and they had added an extra slot to her age group. Now she too was in with a realistic chance of getting a Kona slot. The second surprise was that my age group had lost one slot and now only had six.

The provisional allocation of Kona slots is based on the number of entrants in each age group but is only confirmed by the number of starters on race day, it's calculated on the number of people in each category who actually show up and race. There is always a drop- out rate between entering and race day because of the fact that you have to enter most Ironman races a year in advance.

Aisling's category was up first and it was over quickly, like pulling a sticking-plaster off a cut. There were two slots, both of which were accepted, with no roll down. I could see the disappointment in her face and the way she slumped when she heard the news. All her hopes were gone in an instant, to be replaced with a feeling of failure. I think she was surprised at just how bad she felt to have almost had it . . . to be so close she almost could touch it, and then to have it snatched away.

My age group was up next and they said there was one slot not accepted and that it would roll down. My stomach lurched and I thought I might be sick. I was sweating with the stress and tension. I'd hoped for two slots to roll and I would be in. The next couple of seconds seemed to just drag on and on. Then they called the name of the seventh place finisher as the first candidate for the slot and he immediately jumped up ecstatic and accepted.

Just like that it was over and I slumped in my chair, sick and sore and more disappointed than I'd ever been at a result. It was made so much worse by the emotional roller coaster we'd been on since the race finish. It was the most incredible high and most emotional finish I'd ever had. There was the massive relief and feeling of accomplishment at having achieving what I'd been told I couldn't do and the dawning realisation of what I'd done. I had beaten some of the pro men and women and raced faster than I had ever believed possible.

This was then followed by the feeling that I'd been kicked in the stomach when I found out I hadn't actually qualified. The athlete tracker being wrong, the sleepless night and the long morning of waiting and hoping, and then finishing with the bitter disappointment of both of us missing out by the tiniest margin. One place and only two minutes in a race that took almost then hours. In the end two minutes made the difference between a dream realised or not.

We stayed for the rest of the awards ceremony and then started the journey home. The drive back to the ferry was full of talk, first of the ups and downs of the last twelve hours but this was gradually replaced by our usual race dissection. Each of us took turns to tell our stories from the day and to analyse our performances. We talked about mistakes made and the highlights of the day. These animated discussions are one of my favourite parts of race weekends.

Emotionally I swung from the fear at having to go home and admit I'd failed, to anger, disappointment and self- recrimination. Seventh place was only two minutes ahead of me. I could have hurt myself more and found that two minutes if I'd been willing to work harder or suffer more. Just one place, just two minutes, I kept thinking.

Ais told me the story of her race and I told her about mine and over the course of the next few hours I started to feel differently inside. Swim, bike and run PB's and going over an hour faster than my next best Ironman time became the focus of the day rather than the awards ceremony and missing out on Kona. The negative emotions were replaced with growing feelings of satisfaction, joy and accomplishment. I didn't feel like the dreamer any more who had put an impossible target out there only to fail. I felt like a Kona athlete. I didn't feel like a failure. I hadn't qualified this time but now I knew I could. I believed it deep down inside. It was another one of those pivotal moments in life. . . another switch flicked in my head. I not only believed I could do it – I became that person in my head. I became a Kona person. I would go to Kona, but just not this year. I've never looked at the seemingly impossible in the same way since.

Ironman Florida was next in November, just over three months away. That seemed like plenty of time to try to find that extra two minutes.

CHAPTER 17
NOT SO INVINCIBLE AFTER ALL

After Ironman UK, Aisling and I had a couple of smaller races lined up which were really just for fun. The first was a tweve-hour mountain bike race that we had participated in the previous year and enjoyed very much. The only problem was it was on six days after Ironman UK, so maybe it wasn't the cleverest idea. My sporting background is cycling and mountain biking was how I got started, so I tend to dip my toe into some form of MTB racing or event every year or so and I usually get a fairly rude awakening. Although I'm a bit fitter than when I raced as a beginner, technically I'm dreadful, through lack of practice. This is not a big issue if you are only racing for fun you might think, but it's the lack of ability that turns mountain biking into a contact sport.

After a couple of hours racing and a couple of minor crashes while getting back up to speed, I was gaining confidence when it suddenly started to rain. I continued to push harder, ignoring the couple of little warnings

I got from the slippery trail, until I dropped down onto a wooden bridge crossing a stream and the front wheel went from under me and I ended up face down into the stream after bouncing off the bridge. Feeling a bit shook- up I decided that I was going to go a bit easier and not risk breaking something and missing out on months of training. We finished the race without any more major incidents, both of us happy to have survived and not too keen to go into an event so under-prepared again.

The following Tuesday saw a return to a normal week's swim training and myself and Ais were back running and biking before the weekend. On Saturday we raced a sprint triathlon and a bike race on the Sunday. This is where I started to make my second big mistake after Ironman UK. I was starting to feel recovered and my confidence was growing after almost every training session. My swim times were coming down almost every time I got into the pool and I had broken my best times in training for 1500m and 3800m twice in two weeks. I was doing longer and harder sessions and running faster and stronger and biking better almost every time I went out. I was starting to feel invincible and was pushing harder and harder in training. Both Ais and my coach tried to slow me down but I had momentum and wanted to see more improvement.

I took his programme and added more sessions, hitting thirty hours in the third week of August – less than a month after Ironman UK. The height of my stupidity was doing a 200k bike ride and a hard ten-kilometre run off it. The session had me down to do two or three hours at Ironman pace and the rest easy. Instead I did the whole thing at race pace, going through 180k in just over five hours then running the ten kilometres in a little over forty minutes, feeling like I could have gone on for another hour like that. If I had those legs on race day I probably would have won my age group in Ironman UK, I thought. I'd never felt so strong, I just couldn't contain it.

I added another three long bike sessions to the week's training my coach had given me on top of his programme, as I had a long weekend off work. I was convinced I knew better. By Saturday I was cooked. I went from feeling like a superhero to not wanting to get out of bed and cutting every session short. Like a bubble being burst . . . I popped.

Ais and the coach could see I was overdoing it but I had been blinded by my enthusiasm and progress and kept on looking for more and more. Motivation went from 100% to zero in a matter of days and my energy levels followed suit. I was exhausted all the time and skipping sessions. Over the next month I only averaged about ten hours training per week. It didn't help that it felt like we were the only two people in Ireland still thinking about racing. The season was over and everyone was talking about taking a break and enjoying their off season.

I was then starting to panic. Ironman Florida was only six weeks away and I wasn't getting back to earlier levels of training or fitness and my motivation was still the lowest it had been all year. I couldn't face doing the long solo time trial bike rides or the four and five-kilometre swims that I was supposed to do. I wasn't looking forward to the race and was regretting entering an event so late in the season. It was very different to the run-in for any race I'd done before in terms of the pressure I felt to perform well for myself and all the people who supported me throughout the year.

October finally saw me turn a corner in terms of training and I started to string together a couple of good days and then a week and momentum started to build again. I got three solid weeks of training done, but I was still missing what for me was a key ingredient: I hadn't done any long quality bike sessions. In preparation for Ironman this is fairly critical as the bike is at least half and usually quite a bit more of the race time. It also hugely affects how well you run the marathon. It was too late now to do anything about that as there were only two weeks to go to the race. I tried to forget about it and get on with the last bit of race preparation.

The other thing missing that I had had in the UK was the confidence that comes from knowing that I had all the training done. I found this tough to deal with mentally and it affected my last couple of days before the race. The fire I had to go and race hard just wasn't there and nothing I was doing seemed to get it back. I would have to hope that the excitement of race day would sort that problem out.

CHAPTER 18
IRONMAN FLORIDA 2011

Race morning came and it was colder on the beach than in the water. I wasn't as relaxed as I was at IMUK. I was more apprehensive about my performance than the race distance. It's funny how in only three Ironman races it's gone from being just finishing the race distance that was the challenge to being a distance that I now really wanted to race. I lined up at the edge of the beach about two rows back as I still wasn't confident about my swim. The gun went and I ran straight in with the huge charge and surge of bodies.

It instantly turned into the hardest, roughest, most physical swim I've ever done. Almost 3000 people, all looking to get as close as possible to the first buoy meant it was crazy. Although the sea was flat we were also fighting with very strong currents, pushing us across the course. I was swum over, punched, kicked and had my goggles knocked off. It felt suffocating at times and I didn't think I'd find any clear water at all. The whole first lap was chaos. Despite all that, I mostly enjoyed it once I got over the initial panic. I quite enjoy rough swims, but I'm just not very good at them. I'm too light and I don't have the strength and power that a real swimmer would have.

In Florida you run up onto the beach halfway through the swim in what's called an Australian exit and then head back out for the second lap and it had started to spread out at that stage. It also gave me a chance to see where I was in the field. I'd hoped to get out of the swim just inside the top 100, but there looked to be an awful lot of people in the water ahead of me. The second lap was a lot more swimming and a lot less fighting and again I really enjoyed it. I raced without a watch so I had no idea of my time until afterwards, which was probably just as well as I was over six minutes slower and more than 300 places further back than I had hoped. So not knowing my time then was a good thing I reckon. Exiting the water I was just inside the top 400, leaving myself with a massive task to get into at least the top 50.

Swim 1:06:55

Transition 1 was also slower than planned by about two minutes. I just couldn't get it together. I was like a cabbage, fumbling slowly through making mistakes and dropping things. I thought: 'bring on the bike, and quickly'.

Transition 1: 6:59

Biking had gone really well for me that year and despite the patchy training leading into this race (this is always both my favourite and strongest leg) I was looking forward to it. I felt good and straight away started passing people and immediately started moving up the field. The Ironman Florida bike course is pancake flat, the only 'climb' is a motorway overpass and the road surface for the most part is great. This leads not only to fast bike splits but also to lots of drafting, made worse today by strong headwinds as many of the racers hid on wheels, looking for shelter. The wind seemed to turn with us and we only had a tail wind for a short time late in the bike leg.

I raced aggressively on the bike, pushing harder than I would normally, trying to pass and stay away from the packs of drafting riders. In Ironman triathlon you aren't allowed to ride less than ten metres behind another bike, as you will gain an advantage as the rider in front is breaking the wind. The difference in effort riding in a pack is about twenty to thirty per cent less for the rider being sheltered. This means you can ride a lot faster for less effort. It happens often in Florida because there aren't any hills to break up the packs, and there were a lot of packs. It drove me nuts and I let rip a couple of times at guys trying to cheat and sit on my wheel. I surged and pushed to break away from them and would ride away solo for a couple of minutes before the pack would just ride back by me. I went again and again. I was feeling strong and the anger led to me riding a lot more aggressively and much harder than normal.

I remembered some advice I got from a guy who had raced Florida before. He said he just sat ten to fifteen metres off the back of a pack when they caught and passed him and waited for a draft marshal to catch them. Then when they were penalised and the group broke up he would go back past them.

I decided to try the same tactic and let them past the next time they caught me. As the pack of about twenty to thirty riders passed, I let the gap open up to about ten or fifteen metres and rode steadily, matching their pace. It didn't take too long before a motorbike marshal pulled up alongside me and matched my pace. I nearly got sick, thinking I was about to be penalised and checked my distance. I was way back and I looked over at the marshal sitting on the back of the bike. She smiled at me and kept on taking down the numbers of the pack.

When she had them all she tapped her driver to move up and she proceeded to show all of the pack the drafting card. They would have to make a stop at the next penalty tent and wait there for a number of minutes as a result. She made sure the pack split and rode at the legal distance before heading off. I picked up my pace as the riders in front slowed, without the benefit of the pack and picked them off one at a time. Close to half way through the bike I knew that I couldn't keep riding as hard and surging like I had been or I'd blow up.

At the turnaround point I would have a chance to count the competitors in front of me as they went in the opposite direction. There were still a lot of small packs riding together and I got more and more angry seeing this cheating. I had hoped to be inside the top fifty at this stage but as the numbers climbed past 110 I stopped counting and I could see any chance of a Kona slot slipping away. I decided that I would have to treat it as a run race now because I was so far back. I continued to push but rode a little steadier to the end of the bike. I was very sore and much more tired than I'd expected, most likely as a result of riding as hard as I did for the first half of the bike.

Bike 5:05:44

T2 was another fumble fest and worryingly my legs didn't seem to be working.

Transition 2 - 2:46

Then it was on to the run and I was pushing to find a rhythm with a sense of panic and anger overcoming me. Kilometres one, two and three saw me catching and passing a half dozen guys, but it felt very hard. I was intent on running down as many of those in front of me as I could, and to hell with caution, I was going to go hard all the way. My anger pushed but my legs were not co- operating at all. Then all of a sudden at about the five kilometre mark something clicked and I started moving really well. Picking off runners one after another and I started to feel really good – in fact the best I'd felt all day. I found that groove that I knew I could hold onto for a long time. I would look up the road and pick my next target and hunt them down. I also smiled at all of the spectators and started saying 'well done' to everyone as I passed. Some responded and some were too far inside their own heads to notice but the ones who did gave me a lift and the smiles and cheers from the crowd pushed me on. I was passing people all the way through the first lap and moving up through the field. I was careful to eat, drink and cool myself with the sponges at all the aid stations.

I continued to feed off the crowd and the other competitors using their encouragement to keep me moving. This is something Ais taught me and

I find it gives me a huge boost. Onto the second lap and the course was filling up and the buzz was growing. At about the thirty kilometre mark I was still flying. I felt fantastic and was catching and passing some of the pro men. This was despite the fact that they had started ten minutes before the age group race. I got a huge lift from this and it pushed me on more. It wasn't until thirty five kilometres that it began to really hurt and I started slowing a bit.

Like Ironman UK the pain went from just being like background noise to being front and centre and feeling like a lot of pain almost instantly, but I didn't care. I knew that I had less than half an hour to go and I kept telling myself that I could hurt for that long. I had thought and hoped I would see Ais on the course but the way the lap in Florida is set out I never did. I ran harder and pushed all the way. Just like IMUK the support from the crowd was fantastic, especially when they saw that I was on my last lap, heading in to finish.

One of the best feelings of the race was as I came to the end of the lap and there was a marshal directing people back out for the start of their next lap and as I caught his eye I smiled as big a smile as I had all day pointing straight ahead indicating I was finishing and he gave me a huge shout and a high five as I ran by, knowing the pain was nearly over.

There was about a kilometre to go to the finish and I looked up to realise there was a guy just ahead that I might still catch. I couldn't believe I was about to start sprinting again at the end of an Ironman with nine-and-a- half hours racing completed and legs feeling like lead. I put my head down and I surged hard and tried to hold on to the speed. When I looked up he was walking. I couldn't believe my luck. I pushed harder and looked up again. He was running again but I was gaining fast. One more surge and I had him. I passed him fast, hoping he was too tired to respond. I held the pace for another ten seconds and backed off a bit but didn't dare look back. After a second I could hear footsteps and looked back to see if I was being chased by someone else. I couldn't believe it. I surged again and again but he was still there. I could hear his feet slapping and him breathing hard on my shoulder. I was sprinting all out and still couldn't see the finish. I pushed again and thought he was fading behind and gave it one last surge coming into the finish chute at last – to a huge cheer. The crowd loves a sprint finish.

I held him off in the end by a couple of seconds. I turned immediately and as with all triathlons I've done the guy you were trying to kill ten seconds ago is the first one over to shake hands and congratulate you. It's one of the best parts of the sport.

Run 3:18:37

Overall 49th 9:40:29

After getting my finisher's T-shirt and medal I headed straight to the food tent. I was starving, and started into slice after slice of pizza and bottles of water while I was waiting for Ais to finish. I met and held her after she crossed the line. The end of an Ironman is always very emotional for me and it's only made that much better if you get to share it with someone you love and admire.

In the end I had moved up from almost 400th out of the swim to 110th off the bike to forty-ninth overall and eleventh in my age group after the run. This was not enough for a Kona slot but I think I got the race I'd trained for, so I wasn't as disappointed as I was in the UK earlier that year. I also learned a lot and really enjoyed it. There were parts of the race that I was happy with and it was a run that I was proud of. I was also happy with my bike time, considering the training mistakes made leading into it. One of the big positive effects on me was mental. It reinforced my belief in myself that I can race at this level and that IMUK wasn't a fluke or a 'soft' race. Again, t h e s a t i s f a c t i o n i n m y d a y o u t w e i g h e d t h e disappointment in not getting a slot for Kona. I also took some more valuable lessons away about race day and the lead into it.

CHAPTER 19
OFF SEASON, ULTRA, HALF IRON

I was mentally exhausted after Ironman Florida and ready for a complete break from structured training for what was left of November and on into December of 2011. After two weeks of doing nothing we started back running. Aisling and I have tended to go back to running whenever we are either in triathlon off-season or taking a break from structured training. I also made contact with a new coach, a guy called Bill Black. He was recommended to me by one of the top Irish Ironman athletes and multiple Kona finisher, Matt Molloy. I was scheduled to start to work with him in January. He was based in the UK, so all contact would be on the phone or by email.

The first month back into proper training for us is very much about seeing how it's going to fit into our life and in forming new routines. I was also starting to incorporate Bill's plan. We were both sort of feeling each other out I suppose initially. The first three weeks on his programme made it obvious that he was going to drive me hard. I was excited and often nervous getting the week's schedule and reading what he had planned for me. There was a lot of challenging sessions from the start.

At the end of January we went on a holiday/training camp, but without the bikes. We ran twice most days and I had my biggest swim and run weeks with close to 180k running and 20,000m in the water. Training numbers overall for January weren't massive but I'd put in a lot of swimming and while the bike hours were very low, most of the sessions had a lot of quality work in them –either strength work or intervals. The run was close enough to target and again had plenty of good quality sessions.

January
Total hours 67:30 45 sessions
S 15:15 48600m 16 sessions
B 25:15 716k 10 sessions
R 27:05 295k 19 sessions

I wasn't feeling great at all in February and all month I was missing sessions. I only got about sixty per cent of the scheduled work done. I was constantly tired and, if I'm honest, it was probably due to the one race I did. It was a fifty-kilometre ultra marathon which I think had much more of a negative effect on the month than I would have liked to admit. I did a very short taper and ran it strictly as a long training run and stuck to the pace the coach set. I had a target time of four hours and came in at 3:57.

I still think it took at least two weeks to recover from this, despite running easy. In hindsight it's probably better to do an event like this before I start full training. Any benefit gained from the experience of running that long is far outweighed by the loss of training hours and quality overall during the period. I also started to introduce some strength and conditioning which I was hoping would become an important core part of my training.

February 12
Total hours 55:50 41 sessions
S 13:50 40800m 12 sessions
B 20:05 549k 9 sessions
R 18:05 225.5 13 sessions
S&C 2:40

March was slightly more consistent and I gradually saw an improvement in times and particularly in the quality of the bike sessions. I was still, however, about fifteen hours short for the month's target. Work was getting busier and as usual training was the first thing to suffer. The bike was really the only one of the three that was on target that month, with the swim and run both coming up short. The strength and conditioning was also falling off a bit.

March 12

Total hours 65:20 38 sessions

Swim 8:20 26400m 9 sessions

Bike 47:00 1220k 25.95kph 20 sessions

Run 8:50 102.5k 11.46kph 8 sessions

S&C 1:10

In April things finally started to click and I strung together some good big weeks. But probably the best lesson from the previous three months was that all the training sessions, even those that one doesn't think are working add up over time. I believe Ironman is all about the big picture. The small details like which type of session I should do or how I feel on any given day is much less important than getting the training done consistently. Again the bike volume was close to bang on target, with the swim and run very close to what was scheduled. The improvement in weather helped a lot in getting in the bike miles and a return to club racing for the first time in a number of years. This brought on my bike speed very quickly as well as helping to sharpen up my handling.

The strength and conditioning was miserably poor, only getting in one session for the month.

April 12

Total hours 74:00 46 sessions

Swim 11:40 36600m 16 sessions

Bike 44:40 1211k 15 sessions

Run 15:40 191k 12 sessions

S&C 0:30

Despite work being very hectic in May, I was not only getting good consistent weeks in at the start of the month. I was starting to see my splits improve. I could feel the fitness coming on and with it some confidence. It was the beginning of the triathlon season for me and I was starting with a half Ironman. The other big event was the Race The Ras, an eight-day sportive I rode the previous year which was on again this year. Swim volume for the month was very low, the run wasn't too far off target but with the bike week the volume of cycling was high. The strength and conditioning was still very poor, again only doing one session for the month.

May 12

Total 73:15 32 sessions

Swim 6:40 18300m 6 sessions

Bike 55:10 1627k 16 sessions

Run 15:40 175k 13 sessions

S&C :40

Tri an Mhi 2012 half Iron distance

This was the most nervous and reluctant I've been before any race I can remember. I was dreading the cold of the swim. I'd been hearing stories of freezing open water swims and hypothermia all week and it had got to me. I was battling in my head with a 'why the hell am I doing this' back and forth argument for the last thirty minutes before being herded into the lake. I never used to mind the cold but one of the side effects for me of all the training was that I had become very lean. During race season I usually only have about six to seven per cent body fat, which means I really feel the cold.

The cold was shocking and my chest tightened. I swam a few strokes and stood up. I tried again with the same result. I found it really hard to breathe and we were due to start any second. The starter's gun went and I dived in and had to keep alternating swimming with my head up out of the water then back in to try to get used to the shock. After a couple of minutes thinking I would never get going properly, I gradually adjusted to it and settled into a steady hard rhythm. It wasn't long before I was actually enjoying myself.

My swimming had been improving steadily over that year. In particular my sighting was getting better so I tended not to wander around too much. The first lap went well.

Halfway into the second lap the cold really hit me hard and I started shivering badly. I knew I was in trouble as I slowed more and more. I was aware that I was getting dangerously cold and I was still a couple of hundred metres from shore. I couldn't bend my arm properly to catch the water and as a result slowed further still. I was told afterwards that the lethargy and lack of panic are symptoms of hypothermia. I was being passed by lots of people but couldn't do anything about it as my body began to shut down more and more. I finally made it to the slipway and had to be helped to my feet. I headed into transition but I was so cold that I again needed help. I couldn't put on my jacket and gilet. I was over ten minutes behind the first swimmers out of the water and near the back of the field. I think I was somewhere about 130th place.

Swim 0:39:06

Transition 1– 02:45

It took ages to get going up on the bike. I was shivering violently and tried to push hard to warm up but my body wouldn't respond and I found myself in the unusual position of getting out at the back of the swim and going further backwards. The bike is where I normally start to move up the field and pass people. It took almost thirty kilometres before I warmed up and finally started to go well. From then on I moved steadily up the field all the way through the rest of the bike section. I ended up with a big negative split on the bike, going over seven minutes faster on the second forty-five-kilometre lap when I finally warmed up. I never would have believed that a cold swim could cost so much time overall. I had no idea how far back I was at this stage but I had plenty of racing aggression from the bike and I was going to carry it out onto the run.

Bike 2:51:41

Transition 2 – 00:58

Running out of T2 my feet hit the ground like concrete blocks. Every step hurt, they were so numb with the cold.

I came out of transition pushing hard from the start of the run, throwing caution to the wind. I had nothing to lose by taking a chance and racing hard. I went through the first four kilometres at under four minutes per kilometre pace, which was way faster than I'd planned on starting and much faster than I'd ever gone before – close in fact to my sprint distance race pace. I was going much faster than I thought was sensible to make up as many places as possible, but I decided to keep going until I was forced to slow.

It took about six kilometres to become comfortable on the run but when I got going I really relaxed and enjoyed it. I found a groove and slotted myself into it. I was catching and passing people the whole way and getting a big buzz from it. It was a hilly run which tends to suit me and I moved steadily up the field. The run was by far the highlight of the day for me, finishing only four minutes off my stand-alone half marathon pb (that despite the fact that the run course at twenty two kilometres is actually a little long) and running hard all the way. It was a good lesson, where I discovered that I could go much harder than I could have thought if I was willing to hurt myself.

Run 1:27:08

Overall 17th. Age Group 3rd 5:01:40

Despite the problems with the cold I felt I was coming into very good shape and my confidence was good.

CHAPTER 20
RACE THE RÁS 2012 –
PROLOGUE: PRE-RACE RITUALS

There are a number of rituals that I go through before every big race or event. At this stage they are almost like superstitions.

Carb loading

This is my favourite part of the build-up to any big event, and in the case of the Race the Rás I continue to load carbs for ten whole days, including two days before the start and every day during the event. Afterwards I keep on eating huge amounts, as the metabolism is running so hard it's like a furnace. Everything I put in is incinerated instantly and as a consequence cries out for more.

Bike check and cleaning

In the last couple of days before a race I love to clean and prepare my bike. Even though I have it serviced in the workshop a week before, it's now a part of my routine to strip and clean it myself, usually replacing bar tape, cables and tyres. I also fine-tune the gears and brakes so they are absolutely perfect. I leave nothing to chance. For Race The Rás I pack a week's worth of spares, an extra wheel set and a tool box . . . just in case. The last thing I pack for the bike is a packet of baby wipes so I can clean it after each day. I don't do that much hands-on work on bikes in the shop anymore. I just don't have the time but it's a real passion of mine to work on high-end bikes. I find it very therapeutic and relaxing and this is one part of the preparation I really enjoy.

Packing

Packing is my least favourite thing and the most stressful part of race preparation, so as a result it's usually the last thing to be done. We have to work off a list (and when I say 'we' what I really mean is Aisling) we have compiled over a couple of years so we don't forget anything.

Resting up

I normally have at least one day of complete rest before a big race. This is often spent in a hotel or in the camper van. When we travel to races I try to spend the day flat on my back, surrounded by snacks, drinks and books. In this case because Race The Rás is eight days long, the week leading up to it is manic in work, trying to get ahead of myself – so Saturday is spent in the shop. It's not perfect preparation, but neither is it the end of the world.

Depending on how big an event is and how my preparation has gone, these things either settle my nerves or make me more nervous. This time I'm feeling calm and confident even though the RTR is a huge week, covering over 1200km in eight days. Over the last while the body has started to come around and I'm starting to feel strong. Even with work getting very busy for the last month or so I'm meant to have had two slightly lower volume-training weeks and I'm fairly well rested going into it.

Another plus is that it's not the big unknown that it was last year, so it's much less stressful. Maybe I'm remembering it through rose-tinted glasses, but I'm really looking forward to it. The camaraderie develops over the week of spending five or six hours a day pedalling with a gang of riders that start off being strangers and end up being your 'best mates ever'. I hoped the weather would be kinder to us this year after the epic conditions we had last year. Aisling isn't riding this one as she is in the middle of training for a 24-hour ultra marathon in July.

This is one of my most important training weeks of the year. There is nowhere else that I can ride in a group with support for five to six hours every day for eight days, covering up to 190km a day. It's perfect Ironman training for me as I find my bike fitness transfers well to the run and I seem to be able to absorb the huge volume and recover fairly quickly.

From the first day I knew I was in good shape and I had decided that I would ride hard as much as possible. I was quite happy to push hard all day, every day, and arrive at the finish exhausted, but knowing that I could spend the afternoon recovering and eating, so I was ready to go again the next day. I wanted the whole week to be a huge overload, when I could recover properly afterwards. I felt so good on several of the days I added twenty to thirty kilometres onto the end of the ride to bring my mileage up close to 200k a couple of times. Other days I ran about ten kilometres off the bike but I only got in one swim. I felt stronger and stronger as the week went on and I rode more aggressively as a result. I took a huge amount of confidence from the event as well as the massive training benefits.

CHAPTER 21
IRONMAN UK (IMUK), JULY 2012

Every journey begins with a first step. That journey's first step was Aisling's belief that I could do it and her convincing me to believe in myself when nobody else, including myself, believed I could succeed.

Last year that race was the closest thing to an easy Ironman I had done and I almost qualified for the World Championships in Kona at my first attempt. That gave me the idea that I would again cruise through it in 2012. Having greater fitness, coupled with the fact that I was moving into a new age group, surely I would comfortably land a Kona slot and possibly a podium place too? I went into this one thinking it was in the bag. I was about to learn that Ironman doesn't give an 'easy' ride to Kona, so I was in for a very rude awakening.

All the racing and training for the last six months had built really well. I had been setting new swim pb's at every distance from 100, 200 and 400 metres all the way to 4 kilometres. My speed and strength had both improved hugely. My biking was going better than ever before by a long way. I'd been feeling so much stronger and confident as a result and a return to bike racing had added an element of sharpness and speed that hadn't been there previously.

The run was the only area that I didn't think had improved hugely, but I believed that if I could hold on to my form from the last two races, added to my much greater overall fitness, I wouldn't have any problem running a fast time. It's only a marathon after all. . . Like I said I was confident.

Race week came and the magic, strong feeling that had been in my legs for weeks was gone. I had no idea how to get it back and without it my confidence was faltering. All season I had been getting better on the bike in particular and now with two days to go my legs decided it was time for a siesta. I did an hour on Thursday before the race on the bike, nice and steady with just a couple of efforts at race pace. It felt ok but not quite right. On Friday I headed out again, hoping my legs had just gone to sleep after a couple of easy weeks on the bike and I tried to convince myself they were back, that once again I had that magic feeling of being able to hit the gas and hold it for ages, then hit it again and again. But it wasn't there. I felt like I was stuck in third gear, revving the engine like crazy, but I couldn't find fourth, never mind fifth or sixth. I was getting more and more nervous and worried but there was nothing to do now but hope that my legs would wake up before Sunday for the race. Aisling reassured me all was well. The training was done and I was just being paranoid – and she was usually right.

But a big part of me thought that time that she was wrong.

Sunday. Race day

I've not been this nervous before a race for as long as I can remember. I'm queuing for a Portaloo with Aisling and I'm not talking much. I am trying to relax but all I can hear is this guy behind me with the most annoying voice on the planet who won't shut up. 'This is a long queue. How long do you think it'll take to get to the start? I need to use the toilet. Do you think it's gonna rain? It might get hot today but not as hot as my last race. That was really hot. I don't think it'll rain.'

Jesus I wanted to kill him. Shut up man. I'm not usually this nervous and I'm much more irritable than usual. Making my apologies to Aisling I put in my headphones and stuck on my race day playlist, bringing instant relief. It's just me in my head and I start to settle down. I have my eyes closed and I'm starting to get into race mode. Then I get a tap on the shoulder and I open my eyes expecting Aisling, but it's my parents and my brother, who have spent all night driving and travelling on the car ferry from Dublin to Holyhead to come and surprise me and to watch me race. I'm speechless, but delighted. After a couple of minutes chatting it's time to get into the wetsuit and then into the water.

The swim

I'd rehearsed this swim in my head dozens of times over the last twelve months, visualising myself sighting well and getting into a good strong group to set a new pb. I was hoping to get out of the water in just under the hour. Normally my arms hurt with the fast race start for about ten minutes but then as they warm up I settle and the pain eases into discomfort and I then settle into a fast rhythm. But no matter how hard I tried I couldn't find that groove and the swim was hard, sore and uncomfortable from start to finish. . . not to mention very slow. I tried telling myself that it was a long course or slow conditions and that everyone else would have a poor time, but I didn't really believe it.

Swim: 1:08:44 204th

T1 4:05

T1 went well and I got out quickly onto the bike. It was time to find out if my legs were back. I was less than two kilometers into the bike when my rear tyre blew out. I was just entering a roundabout and was lucky to stay upright as I leaned into the turn. I tried not to panick as I quickly changed tubes but athletes were streaming by me. Dozens of them, maybe hundreds. I tried hard to control myself as I restarted and not chase the lost minutes spent at the side of the road.

Unlike last year when I started very conservatively, I rode a little harder and I was moving up the field constantly, passing other riders. I was going well but it felt much harder than usual. The bike normally takes me anything up to an hour of discomfort and sore legs before I settle into a groove. I often find that it sometimes helps to hit a climb at around this stage. I think it's the change of position from being seated and in the tri bars to getting out of the saddle for the climb that seems to wake them up.

As it happens in IMUK the first climb comes at about an hour for me and I was looking forward to stretching my legs on it. However, from the start I realised I didn't have the usual zing. I wasn't climbing well. It felt like very hard work and I had run out of gears already. This was only a couple of hundred metres into the hill, which was not a good sign. I was trying not to panic, hoping that I would eventually settle into my rhythm. After the climb and descent I got to my favourite part of the bike course. It was a really fast 15km and I was moving well but still not feeling strong.

I didn't really know what was wrong. My legs felt dreadful and were sore no matter what I did. I tried slowing down, speeding up, eating more, eating less and drinking more to see if it helped, but nothing had any effect. I eventually just gave up trying to fix it and accepted that I didn't have good legs for the bike. Despite my difficulties I was still moving through the field. At about three hours in I started cramping a bit and had to make a decision. I knew how badly I wanted to qualify. What I needed to decide was how much I was willing to risk and how much I could hurt myself and keep moving.

I could try backing right off to sort out the legs. Let them recover and probably lose twenty or thirty minutes on the bike? There was no way I would make up that much with even a savage run, so that wasn't an option. I could continue to push, knowing I was damaging my legs for the run. It wasn't really a choice. I had to keep pushing despite the pain and hope my legs wouldn't be too wrecked for the run.

I caught up with Irish pro Eimear Mullen who was in second place in the women's race, close to the end of the bike and gave her a shout. I estimated she wouldn't be long catching me on the run. I finished the bike in 5:34, moving up to sixty-first overall and sixth in my age group, although I wouldn't know that for another hour or so when Aisling updated me on the run course.

It's worth noting that even with a slower than expected swim, a puncture and what felt was a dreadful bike, I was at this stage still in a qualifying position.

Bike 5:34:32

T2 1:16

I got through T2 quickly, taking just over a minute. The first kilometre out of transition was mostly downhill, so it usually helped to get the legs turning over, while finding a rhythm. They were bad from the start, feeling really sore and cramped. I've had sore legs before at the start of an Ironman marathon, but they came good, giving me a decent run split, so didn't panic. Matt Molloy, one of the top Irish age group Ironman racers was on the course offering support. He kept on telling me I was moving well and to keep it up. I felt really guilty for letting my head drop and for feeling sorry for myself. Allowing the support to lift me I decided to try to focus on enjoying the run and not on how bad I was feeling. Very gradually I found a rhythm and although it was slower than I'd hoped, I kept on pushing. At about the 15k mark I saw Aisling and my family again. She was shouting that I was still moving up the field and was into the top 50 now and was sixth in my age group getting off the bike. It was the first time I'd had any real idea about where I was and it gave me a huge mental lift to know I was still in with a chance of getting a qualifying slot for Hawaii.

One of the biggest motivations for me not to give up was to know how important it was to other people. Aisling had been there every step of the way and just imagining the shame of having to admit to her the next day that I gave in because it was too hard and hurt too much kept me pushing. I also couldn't stand the idea of letting my family down after taking time out of their lives to come and watch me. There was also the fact that I had announced in a national magazine what I intended to do and there was no way I was writing another article saying I had missed it again. All I needed to do was stay in the top seven, with about 27k to go. I told myself I could hurt for that long.

Less than five minutes later things took a nosedive. I slowed so much I was afraid I'd end up walking. I was hurting more than I ever have in an Ironman and I started to pray that I had a bit of a buffer between myself and the next guy in my age group. I had no sooner thought that than I heard someone move onto my shoulder and he went straight past. I looked down at his leg to check his age group, because we had our category marked on our calves. He was M40 – my age group.

He was going so much faster that there was no chance I could stay with him. There goes seventh I thought. I started praying that he was the last one, hoping that the next one had to be a bit further back. I just need to recover and get moving a bit faster, I told myself. Then another M40 went past at the same speed as the last one. I just cound'nt believe it.

It was normally about that stage that I started to pass people who were in the state that I was in then. I dug as deep as I ever have in a race to get back to him and hung on for dear life. One kilometre passed, then two and three and I was still with him but I was way over my limit. I lasted one more kilometre and then he started pulling away. That's eighth gone, I thought. I can't respond and I can see Kona slipping away. Less than a minute later I lose ninth. I am sorer than I've ever been. My legs are tying up with cramps and every step sends jagged pain shooting through my calves and quads. I lose tenth and then eleventh. I eat and drink at the aid stations, hoping that food might help bring me back around. At last I stop losing places but I'm out of the running completely, now five places off qualifying and only one 10k lap to go.

There's a climb out of Bolton at the start of the lap and just after the steepest part, as I got onto the long drag, I tried again. I pushed and picked up the pace, hoping I could hold on to it. The pain is still massive but this time the legs respond and I hold the increased pace. I can see eleventh place in my age group ahead and I'm closing on him. I dig in and push again, risking it all now. I'm so close to my limit that if I go over it I'll end up walking. At this stage I had nothing, so I'd nothing to lose. I pass him and he doesn't respond. Then I see tenth.

I put my head down and push and catch him and as I do I surge, so he doesn't try to come with me. I hold on to the speed as long as I can and he doesn't come with me. I get to the 5k to go mark and I see ninth. I can see Kona again. I can hurt myself for another five kilometres. I pick up the pace way past what I thought I could sustain and every part of my body is screaming at me to quit and lie down. I've never wanted so badly to just stop. I pass ninth almost sprinting. At least that's how hard it feels. There's no way I can hold this effort to the end but I'm terrified of being caught and I can almost see a slot.

I'm hurting so much now that I can only convince myself to keep pushing for one more minute at a time. I last one minute more and then convince myself to just hold on for one more. I pass the 4k to go point and I'm in so much pain and so focused on pushing for just one more minute I almost miss the M40 mark on the next one's calf as I pass and move into eighth. I dig in harder and he comes with me. I hold onto the speed, hoping he will crack. I'm counting the seconds now, because I can't even think in minutes. He's still there and it's harder mentally to have him there because somehow it makes the suffering worse. So I surge to drop him and he claws his way back onto my shoulder.

I've only got one more push. If he comes back at me he can have it. I surge and hold onto the pain and he comes back again. I give in to the pain. Then I think of Aisling and push again. He comes back again. I surge again and before he can get back I go again and again. I pass the one kilometre to go and the crowd support us with wild cheering and shouting and I try to let it lift me, so I dig in again. I can't hear him but I'm too afraid to look back in case he takes it as a sign that I'm fading and comes back at me. I come around the last few corners onto the cobbled section sprinting. The pain is all consuming but I can see the finishing chute and hear the roar of the crowds. I hold on for another hundred metres and as I turn into the chute I snatch a glance over my shoulder and see there's no one there.

I almost collapse after I stop. I've never had to dig as deep before and I can't stand. I drop onto my knee and hold on to the barrier. I cross the line in eighth place in my age group and 51st overall. There are seven slots in my age group. Again I need someone ahead of me to not accept a slot so it will roll down and again I won't find out until the next morning at the awards ceremony.

Run: 3:40:10

Overall: 10:28:47. 51st Overall. Eighth in Age Group

Initially I'm upset, feeling massive disappointment. I had high hopes coming into this race and all the indications were that I could achieve a higher placing than this. Eventually I realised that even on a bad day I had placed well and the disappointment started to lift.

At the awards ceremony the next morning Aisling and my mother were close to needing Valium because they were so wound up, but I was very relaxed, confident that I had done enough and that a slot would roll down to me. When the announcer got up to the M40 category and said there was not only one but two roll-downs and called my name, the relief washed over me.

I stood up and said I would take the slot and sat back down again, at which point he asked me if I was not going to come up and accept my Hawaii'ian Lei. In my relief I had forgotten that I should go up on stage where it was presented to me. Racing in Kona had been a dream for almost half my life and for the last year it had become an all-consuming passion. It's funny but for the previous twelve months just qualifying had been my target. I had been so focused on this day being the ultimate goal that I hadn't really looked past it. The dawning realisation now was that I needed to start training for another Ironman. So that incredible day was only the beginning of the next chapter.

CHAPTER 22
KONA 2012 –THE TRIP AND RACE WEEK

$\mathbf{A}$fter the underpants run finishes Kona once again returns to a normal level of super weirdness.'
Aaron Hersh - Twitter

The flight from Los Angeles International Airport (LAX) to Kona offered a glimpse of what was going to be one of the strangest experiences I had ever had. It was without doubt the fittest flight I had ever been on. I spotted over 40 triathletes on the flight with us, and they were just the ones that were easy to pick out. They all had some or all of the following:

- Ironman race t-shirt, bag, hat or jacket.

- Ironman tattoo, or several in the case of a couple of guys.

- Shaved legs. (on the guys, although if the girls had hairy legs I assumed they weren't triathletes either)

- Bike brand t-shirt, Trek, Zipp etc.

- Marathon or other race t-shirt

- Wild colour racing flats Newtons, Zoots, Asics Noosa or similar
- Livestrong wristband
- Carry on luggage is a transition bag
- Body fat percentage in single digits
- Carrying a bottle of water, energy drink or bike bottle
- Wildly-coloured Oakleys
- Cyclist tan
- M35s and M40s often as not have a shaved head
- Facial tan with white Oakley-shaped stripe
- Arm tan, stopping at the wrist around the same place as cycling mitts

Thankfully there wasn't anyone wearing calf guards or compression tights. This would have been a dead giveaway, but it was six days to go to the race, so probably that would have been a little bit too early. I ticked a number of the boxes myself but I'll keep which ones to myself.

The first thing that hits you when you land is the heat. Even though it was almost 11pm by the time we landed it felt like it was in the high twenties Centigrade as we walk down the steps. It enveloped us in a way that only happens in really hot countries. The airport terminal was outdoors which gave a good indication of the unlikelihood of rain. We made out way to the outdoor luggage carousel. I was a bit dazed because it was all so surreal. My legs were carrying me but I felt I was really only a passenger going along for the ride. It hit me why I was there as the bike boxes arrived out and were are dumped on the tarmac out at the front of the airport buildings. I got a shiver of excitement, despite the heat. I could not quite believe I was in Kona, less than a week away from racing The Ironman.

Tuesday was our first day in Kailua and it was a real shock to the system. Everywhere we went there was another triathlete riding a €10,000+ bike, running-bare chested, or walking to the beach in Speedos. The difference there to any other race I had been to before was that the whole town was there for the Ironman. Over 5,000 volunteers, 2,000 athletes racing and probably another 10,000 supporters and spectators. That's right – you did read that correctly – there were 2.5 volunteers for every athlete racing. Then there was all of the industry people. All of the big bike companies were there, along with all of the big American triathlon companies for the highlight of Ironman racing for the year. Every shop was selling Mdot and triathlon clothing, souvenirs and accessories. We spotted former World Champion Faris Al Sultan out running in his Speedos just after we arrived into town. Faris is famous for racing in his Speedos and a crop top like what would have been fashionable fifteen or twenty years ago, instead of the more common triathlon shorts or tri suit. It's funny to realise that he trains in them too.

We made our way to the practice swim and as I was getting changed on the front lawn of the King K Hotel I look up to see I'm standing next to four-time World Champion Chrissie Wellington. There are hundreds of the fittest people I've ever seen, all stripping off to reveal six packs, bulging pecs, biceps, quads and calves. It was the most intimidating place you could imagine and I really didn't feel like I belonged there with those people. These were obviously all the fastest and strongest Ironman triathletes from all over the world and I felt like an impostor. I half expected someone to come over, tap me on the shoulder and tell me they made a mistake and that I shouldn't really be there. Nobody did, however, so I made my way onto Dig Me Beach, where there was a tiny triangle of sand at the start of the pier.

I waded in and dived into warm crystal clear blue water and immediately saw dozens of wildly colourful tropical fish swimming below me. I couldn't stop smiling and swam slowly and easily out to the Coffees of Hawaii boat which was about 500 metres from the shore. I had lost all interest in a training swim. I just couldn't stop watching the fish and turtles moving below me as I swam by. I got out to the coffee boat and reached up to hold onto the side of it. One of the girls handed me down a small coffee as I treaded water and held on. It was a very surreal moment in what would turn into a week of weirdness. I reached up for another cup while watching more swimmers arrive. The area around the boat was packed with people treading, water, drinking coffee out of small paper cups. I chatted to a couple of the others in the water and stayed long enough to get a free swim hat and a pair of Speedos.

I reluctantly pushed off from the side of the boat and swam back to the shore where Aisling was waiting. I swam slowly and easily, soaking in every bit of the experience. There were hundreds of swimmers in the water going out to the coffee boat or heading out further on the course for a proper training swim. I never tired of watching the fish and marvelling at how warm and clear blue the water was. After the swim we went for breakfast and on the way met the six-time World Champion Mark Allen. He was happy to stop and talk for a couple of minutes before posing for pictures.

We ate at a restaurant called the Fish Hopper overlooking the swim course and what was to be the finish line in four days. All the time we were there we saw hundreds of swimmers in the water and a constant stream of triathletes, both age groupers like myself and the professionals going past the open front.

I headed out for a spin after breakfast up onto the famous Queen K Highway where I would be racing in a few days. Leaving Kailua the speed rarely dropped below 40kph and it felt easy. Turning back after 50 minutes I was riding into the wind and then the speed dropped. It didn't seem to be as bad as I had read and seen on the TV coverage, but nonetheless it forced me to work hard just to maintain a decent speed.

I met Aisling back in town and we went out to the famous coffee shop and restaurant called Lava Java for lunch and did some more star spotting. All along Ali'i Drive on the way we passed a constant stream of super-fit triathletes walking, running or cycling in or out of town. Every couple of minutes we met another famous current or retired professional and when it seemed appropriate we asked for a picture and chat for a minute about the race on Saturday or about how crazy Kona is. All the people we spoke to were very approachable and happy to chat and spend some time with us. We were surprised to find that they all seemed like completely ordinary people. We had lunch with two of the Irish guys that were racing – Alan Ryan and Martin Muldoon, both of whom had been there before and they gave me some tips for Saturday's race.

Wednesday

We hadn't really adapted to the time difference at that stage and woke early at about 5:15am, when we went out for a short run before heading into town where we again swam out to the coffee boat. The expo was coming to life and the buzz of excitement was even bigger than Tuesday. The highlight of the day for me was the parade of nations. Triathlon Ireland had organised Irish team shirts for all of us. It was an incredibly proud moment walking along in the parade with Aisling and the rest of the Irish team, carrying our national flag. The route was short, only extending from the hotel out about a mile along Ali'i Drive, but it was lined with cheering spectators. I was full of conflicting emotions. I couldn't believe I was there alongside the best in the world. I still didn't feel like I belonged, but I was determined to enjoy every second until someone noticed they had made a mistake and would send me home! After the parade we spent another few hours in the expo, meeting lots of the professionals and buying more gear that we didn't need.

Thursday

I parked outside the supermarket and stepped out of the car. I looked down at myself and stopped – I wasn't wearing any trousers. I stayed behind the open door and looked around. There was nobody there. Ais got out and walked to the back of the car, opened the boot and took out two green leprechaun top hats. She too was wearing only her underwear, consisting of bright green knickers and bra. We were in town early on Thursday for one of the most highly anticipated events of the year – The Kona Underpants Run.

The Underpants run was started as a way to highlight one of the problems caused by Ironman week in Kona. Athletes walking around all day in their speedo's. The culprits were predominantly European athletes but now the speedo tradition is much more widespread. Because it's always close to forty degrees in Kona it's quite comfortable to spend all day in speedo's, even while shopping for groceries. The locals weren't impressed and the underpants run was born to try to allow athletes an outlet for their exhibitionist side while hopefully restricting the public underpants wearing to a single event.

Aisling has spent weeks planning our choice of costume. I was in boxer shorts covered in shamrocks, with knee-high green and white socks, again sporting shamrocks. I had a green glittering bow tie and the leprechaun top hat. I was also wearing a large Irish flag like a cape. I was a six-foot tall super leprechaun in his underwear. Aisling was dressed in a similar vein and had a Pot o Gold basket filled with Irish sweets. We left the car and walked out to the road, waiting to be arrested. People stopped and stared as we walked past. We hadn't really thought out the whole business of getting from the car in our underwear to the run start part of this morning. Maybe we should have brought our tracksuits for the walk down to the town? But it was too late then, so we carried on.

As we arrived down at the pier the crowds were growing and when we turned the corner onto Ali'i Drive we were faced with the sight of almost 2,000 triathletes in their underwear in the street. The week had reached a level of weirdness that is still hard to describe. Taking off almost all your clothes in public isn't unheard of. We have all spent time on a beach in shorts and not thought twice about the lack of clothes, but there's something completely unnatural about walking down the street in boxer shorts. It becomes wildly unreal when you are then surrounded by thousands of others, also in their underwear. Add to that the fact that most of them look fit enough to have just stepped off the front cover of a sports magazine and you are getting close to imagining how crazy it all was.

The pair of us in matching leprechaun outfits is going down really well. We are asked to pose for photos every couple of minutes by spectators, other underwear-clad competitors and even some of the press photographers. We meet up with the rest of the Irish gang and I take the Pot o Gold from Aisling and start handing out sweets to a family walking past, until Aisling points out that a man giving sweets to strange children wearing only a top hat and boxer shorts under other circumstances would get me arrested. I immediately stopped handing out sweets.

The run started a couple of minutes later and I threw sweets at the crowds as we went. It's the craziest, funniest and most enjoyable event imaginable that can be done in a pair of underpants and after doing a loop of the town we finished up back where we started. The crowd gradually dispersed and we made our way back to the car to put some clothes on.

We received tweets and messages all day telling us we made it on to the home page of one triathlon website and into several other triathlon news website photo galleries documenting the morning's antics. It was only Thursday and I couldn't believe we had another four days of this craziness to go through. I went to register and sign on after lunch and the scale of the event started to hit home for me. All of the athletes were being treated like superstars. We were each walked through every step of the sign-on process by a volunteer. They spent as long with me as was needed, patiently answering questions and giving instructions.

My family arrived later that evening and we picked them up from the airport. On Friday morning I swam part of the Ironman course with Dad before breakfast, which was another one of the highlights of the week for me. It was really good of him to come out and swim with me and to experience the warm clear water and the incredible underwater sea life.

Friday was also the day for bike racking and for dropping off my race bags. Again the difference in this race and any other I'd done before was driven home as I went into transition to rack my bike. Everyone was taken through transition by an escort, who walked each competitor to their spots, let them rack their bikes and then explained the flow of transition – where to enter and which way to run. Next they took people to the bag racks, walking them through both the bike and run racking area. This was done individually with every one of the almost 2,000 athletes, the race having over 5,000 volunteers on the spot. That's over twice the number of athletes racing, which is testament to the level of athlete care and attention to detail. Again and again I was amazed at how incredibly far the Ironman organisation went to really look after us. You feel like you are somewhere really special, participating in the most important race in the world, and I still found it hard to believe I was actually part of it. My head was spinning, as I was repeatedly made to feel like a superstar.

CHAPTER 23
IRONMAN WORLD CHAMPIONSHIP, KONA HAWAII 2012

R ace day started for us at 3am, many hours before the race started. We headed into the race area early, as I wanted to not only avoid the last minute rush and queues but I wanted to soak up as much of the atmosphere as possible. First there was body marking, and like every other detail so far this was an experience in itself. Each athlete had people doing the marking, one using a stamp to put each digit on and the other touching up any mistakes with a sharpie marker and a Q-tip. I had two American women doing my numbers and they chatted to me and made sure the numbers were perfectly applied before wishing me luck and sending me on my way. Next came a weigh-in, where my weight was taken and recorded. I then went on into transition to drop off my bottles and food for the bike.

Again I got an intense a sense of the huge occasion it was, with World Champions Craig Alexander and Mirinda Carfrae in transition with all the top professionals. Television cameras and journalists were wandering around and I was trying to soak it all in. I wanted to remember every second of it. I didn't know if I would ever get back there again so I didn't want to forget anything. Once I was sorted I headed out to Aisling and my family. The sun started to come up and the atmosphere and excitement was building. Pretty soon it was time to go to the swim start. The pro men started 30 minutes before us and the pro women were five minutes after them. Then the age group race people started to enter the water.

I waited till about seven or eight minutes before the start and waded in. It was about 200 metres out to the start line and I swam easily, trying to enjoy the buzz, stopping and looking around a couple of times and still not quite believing I was swimming out to the start of the most iconic and famous triathlon in the world.

They fired the cannon to start the race and we were off. It wasn't as rough as some of the other races I've competed in. I was surrounded by good swimmers who were going in the right direction for the most part and I wasn't hit or pushed around too much. I wasn't expecting a fast time. In fact I thought it would be probably one of my slowest IM swims, as it was non-wetsuit. I settled quickly into a rhythm and got into a good group. The first half flew by and we swam around a boat at the furthest point of the course before turning back for home. I was constantly reminding myself to enjoy it. I didn't get much time to check out the extraordinary wildlife swimming around below us because I was sighting and following feet, but every so often a flash of yellow or blue shot past, making me smile.

Thankfully I didn't see any of the sharks Alan Ryan kept telling me were out there. I got out of the water at about 1hr 19. It was a very slow swim by Kona standards, but about where I expected to be. A slow transition followed and then out onto the bike course, passing Aisling and my parents waving Irish tricolours just at the start, which put another big grin on my face. I started conservatively, knowing how hard the bike course is reputed to be. The first couple of hours went fairly well, albeit slower than I had hoped. I wasn't sure if it was the wind or just my legs but I didn't seem to be making my usual progress through the field. I'm used to getting out of the swim down the field and then spending the next couple of hours making my way up towards the front.

That was not happening that day and I had to remind myself that I was competing with the best athletes from all around the world – the top of the age groups from each qualifying race. I hoped that my steady start would see me move up the field later in the day. At the climb up to Hawi we really hit the famous Hawaii winds. It was a hard swirling head and cross wind all the way up the climb, but I was starting to move better getting through the field and I was feeling good. After the turnaround in Hawi it was a wild ride back down to the Queen K Highway with a mixture of screaming tailwinds, switching to harsh crosswinds without warning, which pushed me wildly off line several times on the descent, each time causing a massive blast of adrenaline to course through me.

I was still moving well and able to stay in the tri bars almost all the way. At that stage I started thinking that if I was lucky with the winds on the way back I would actually have a pretty decent time on the bike. I'd started out hoping for about a 5:15 bike split and at that stage it looked like I would be ahead of that. I had reached the 90k mark in just over 2:30. When we got back to the Queen K we turned into a wall of wind and I quickly readjusted my time expectations. The wind was in our faces relentlessly the whole way back and it kept getting hotter and hotter.

My legs were really hurting and I started to fade. I realised I was going to be on the bike for maybe 5:30 and then 5:40. I dug in harder but I started to lose places. I felt like I was going backwards. The wind and heat was harder than I had ever experienced. Everyone had talked about how hard Kona is and I was learning first hand what they meant.

I tried not to get too worried and reminded myself that everyone had the same conditions to deal with. I focussed on enjoying the experience. I reminded myself that it was not every day I rode my bike in Hawaii. Aisling and my parents were again waving the flag and cheering as I came into the last couple of hundred metres and into T2.

After a quicker second transition I headed out onto the run, in boiling heat, with very heavy legs. I had decided the day before to run with a bottle belt for the marathon, but after less than a kilometre I took it off and threw it to my parents after Palani Hill. It took another kilometre before my legs settled and I started to feel good. I moved past people steadily for the first 10k and I was exactly on my target pace. I had decided to start a little slower than I would usually run an Ironman marathon because I was worried about how I would handle the heat. Just after the 11k mark however, I started overheating and slowing down. I told myself not to panic, reassuring myself that I was (sort of) still moving My pace settled at about six minutes a kilometre, a good minute slower than I'd started out at but still an acceptable pace.

I felt I could maintain that speed for as long as it would take. I'd had bad patches in the middle of marathons before and I'd recovered so I felt that if I was careful my legs would come right again.

Heading back into town I knew Aisling would be on the hill at Palani and I planned on stopping and giving her a big sweaty kiss on the way. I knew at this stage that my time was going to be very slow, so I was determined to enjoy it all as much as possible. Kisses done, I high-fived my way all the way up Palani, with great support from the huge crowds and I loved every minute of it. At the top we turned onto the Queen K for the second time that day. We then had 26k of running ahead of us. It only took another mile for things to go very wrong for me and I was reduced to walking the aid stations to fill my hat with ice and take on water and the occasional banana or gel. The end of each aid station was torture in terms of getting going again, but the thought of being out all night kept me running, albeit very slowly.

I was constantly being passed by people in their fifties and sixties. They were very fit-looking 60- year-olds, but still twenty years older than me all the same, which was unbelievably humbling. In the last year I had got myself into the best shape of my life by a long way and there I was falling apart in what was supposed to be my strongest part of the race. Not only was the marathon in particular – but to be honest the whole day – a very humbling experience. I felt like a complete beginner – just like I did at my first Ironman.

I could not believe how hard the race was and how far down the field I was lying. And not just then when I felt like I was falling apart, but also getting out of the swim and seeing more than half of the bikes gone from transition. I didn't get much further up the field on the bike and to top it off I was fading out on the run like I hadn't done in years.

The heat was savage. I filled my hat with ice at every aid station, giving myself an ice cream headache and still it melted way before I got to the next aid station. I repeated the process, threw cups of water over myself and stuffed sponges down the back of my Tri-suit and I was still roasting. It was so hard to keep on running and I still kept telling myself to enjoy it. I would not allow my head to drop or to feel sorry for myself. I asked to be in Kona and there were thousands of people who would have swapped places in an instant, so I didn't allow myself to do anything except to soak it in and try to hang on to as many memories as I could.

At about five miles to go I decided I was going to run all the way, with no more walking in the aid stations and I was going to run it well. I tried to pick up the pace, holding it for about a half-a - mile and then started to slip. But I dug in again and again and the next thing I knew I was at the top of Palani with a blessed downhill and only one mile to go. I picked up the pace before telling myself to run steady. It'll all be over in a couple of minutes I told myself and I wanted to enjoy the last bit.

The time was meaningless at that stage so I continued to soak in the atmosphere. People were cheering and high- fiving all the way in. I couldn'y stop smiling. I stopped to kiss Aisling on the way into the finishing chute and took the Irish flag for the best finish line I've ever experienced. The finishing chute was the longest I've ever done and at the same time not nearly long enough. I wanted the feeling to go on and on. It was the first time I'd carried an Irish flag over the finish of a race and I felt a huge sense of pride. I'm very proud to be Irish, but this was the first time I felt like I earned a finish carrying our national flag – something I never thought I would ever do.

Immediately there was a huge feeling of relief as I crossed the line. It was the first time since my first Ironman that I was afraid of not finishing – afraid of something outside of my control that would end my race early and stop me crossing that line. The pressure for the last couple of races had been in the performance, in the need to qualify. This time I knew that a lot of people were watching me at home. I'd had tons of good luck messages in previous weeks and I didn't want to let anybody down, so the overriding feeling was one of unbridled relief. There was still a part of me that was very disappointed because I was so slow, but I tried not to think about that yet, because there would be plenty of time for that later. For then I just wanted to go on enjoying that wonderful feeling of being in Kona.

CHAPTER 24
BECOMING AN ATHLETE

Before I'd ever taken part in an Ironman, one of the big attractions for me was hearing the many stories describing how it had changed people's lives. For years I'd imagined that when I crossed that line I'd realise a life- changing epiphany – a moment when I would experience a deep life-enhancing revelation.

Of course that didn't happen on the day I crossed my first Ironman finish line in Nice, back in 2008. Ironman isn't magic, it doesn't change you fundamentally in a single moment.

That single moment running down that finishing chute was and still remains with me as one of the most powerful experiences I've ever enjoyed. There weren't any angels hovering around my head whispering the secrets of the universe. Instead, as soon as I crossed the line and stopped moving, a blackness started to descend and slowly and gracelessly I crumpled to the ground.

After I was brought to the medical tent and placed on a fold-out bed with a drip in my arm, I still looked skyward in anticipation, waiting for a flash of something . . . anything.

But that sign failed to materialise, at least not right then. Lying there in the makeshift medical centre I felt a mixture of elation at finishing an event that on the start line I thought might be an impossible task, while there was also a feeling of disappointment that I hadn't found that moment of epiphany. So I hadn't felt a life-changing sensation after all. Having heard all the stories about Ironman changing the lives of people I felt a little cheated then, and if I'm honest about it, that soured the experience for me just the tiniest bit.

It was about a week later when I had given up on having any sort of flash of insight into the meaning of life or the universe that it suddenly hit me. I realised that it wasn't the moment of crossing the finish line of my first Ironman that was the life-changing part. It was the six months of being an athlete leading up to it.

I'd only discovered sport in my late twenties after being a chronically unfit and heavy smoker all of my teenage and adult life. Now, for the first time despite the fact that I had finished in the last 20% of the field, I felt like an athlete. It was the discovery that I loved the discipline required to fit in all the training and that I loved the

feeling and lifestyle of being an athlete. That was the life- changing moment for me.

I made the same assumption years later when I started trying to qualify for Kona – the assumption that I was chasing a moment, a feeling or an epiphany. And again I learned that what I was chasing wasn't a second in time, but a process and an adaptation. For me to take part in Kona I needed to become what I thought of as being a Kona person. I needed to learn how to live the lifestyle of a Kona qualifier. It wasn't just that I had to train more. It was learning how to run a business while training almost full time. It was learning how to find the balance of family and Ironman, while training like a semi-professional athlete.

It wasn't any one single change. When I qualified and then completed the race in Kona (a very similar experience to my first Ironman) there was no moment of revelation as I crossed the finish line. There was just a feeling of deep gratitude that I'd made it, a sense of pride at what we'd accomplished together and the desire to come back and do it better.

Qualifying for Kona for me wasn't an event or a moment. It was changing from being one type of athlete to being another. It was changing from being one type of person to another. It was the realisation that with enough hard work, support and time we may achieve seemingly impossible goals. In many ways getting to Kona for the first time was only the start of my personal journey.

Printed in Great Britain
by Amazon